FOUNDATION GNVQ

Information Technology

Jenny Lawson

Chief Examiner, GNVQ and
Part One GNVQ Information Technology
RSA Examination Board

LONGMAN

Addison Wesley Longman Limited
Edinburgh Gate, Harlow
Essex CM20 2JE, England
and Associated Companies throughout the world

First published 1997

British Library Cataloguing in Publication Data
A catalogue entry for this title is available from the British Library.

ISBN 0–582–29775–3

Set by 30 in Melior 10½/14 and Optima
Printed in Great Britain by Henry Ling Ltd, at the Dorset Press, Dorchester, Dorset

Contents

Introduction

This book is written for Foundation GNVQ Information Technology students.

What is Foundation GNVQ Information Technology?

Foundation GNVQ Information Technology looks at:

- how information technology (IT) is used in industry and commerce
- a range of software applications
- jobs that involve working with IT

How do you achieve an award in GNVQ Information Technology at foundation level?

For the award of a Foundation GNVQ in Information Technology, you must complete nine units:

- three mandatory units from the IT area
- three optional units from any GNVQ area
- three key skills units at level 1

Figure I.1 shows the units for Foundation Information Technology GNVQ.

Evidence of your work will be kept in a **portfolio**. Your understanding of the mandatory units will be assessed in written external tests.

Mandatory units

UNIT 1: INTRODUCTION TO INFORMATION TECHNOLOGY (FOUNDATION)
Element 1.1: Describe uses of information technology
Element 1.2: Describe common applications of information technology
Element 1.3: Demonstrate the use of an information technology system

UNIT 2: USING INFORMATION TECHNOLOGY (FOUNDATION)
Element 2.1: Process documents
Element 2.2: Process graphic images
Element 2.3: Process numerical information
Element 2.4: Process structured data

UNIT 3: INVESTIGATING WORKING WITH INFORMATION TECHNOLOGY (FOUNDATION)
Element 3.1: Examine working with information technology
Element 3.2: Explore jobs that involve working with information technology
Element 3.3: Plan for employment that involves working with information technology

Optional units

UNIT 4: INFORMATION TECHNOLOGY TEAMWORK (FOUNDATION)
Element 4.1: Plan an activity with a team
Element 4.2: Undertake a role in a team activity
Element 4.3: Review the activity

UNIT 5: DOCUMENT PRODUCTION (FOUNDATION)
Element 5.1: Explore common document layouts
Element 5.2: Explore software facilities and hardware for document production
Element 5.3: Create documents

UNIT 6: GRAPHIC DESIGN (FOUNDATION)
Element 6.1: Explore graphics software
Element 6.2: Produce and edit simple drawings using vector-based software
Element 6.3: Produce simple graphic images using bitmap-based software

UNIT 7: MODELLING AND CONTROL (FOUNDATION)
Element 7.1: Describe modelling and control systems
Element 7.2: Use information technology for modelling
Element 7.3: Use information technology for control

UNIT 8: OBTAINING INFORMATION FROM ELECTRONIC SOURCES (FOUNDATION)
Element 8.1: Describe electronic information sources
Element 8.2: Use a public broadcast information service
Element 8.3: Search and retrieve information from a local electronic information database

UNIT 9: INFORMATION COLLECTION AND PROCESSING (FOUNDATION)
Element 9.1: Explore data and information
Element 9.2: Collect and capture data for processing
Element 9.3: Process data and print reports

Figure I.1 **Summary of the units in Foundation GNVQ Information Technology**

You also have to gain the key skills units, but as far as is possible evidence of key skills may be taken from within your portfolio of work for the mandatory units. Your tutor or teacher will advise you on how you can build evidence of key skills into your mandatory assignments.

What is a unit?

A unit covers one area of study. Looking at Figure I.1, Unit 3 concentrates on 'working with information technology'.

Each unit is then split into three or four 'elements' which focus on particular areas of study. For example:

- Element 3.1 examines 'working with information technology'
- Element 3.2 explores 'jobs that involve working with information technology'

and so on.

What is an element?

An element tells you the skills, knowledge and understanding that you need, and what evidence you must produce to prove you have covered the work.

Each element has five main headings:

- performance criteria
- range
- evidence indicators
- amplification
- guidance

Figure I.2 shows the parts of Element 3.1.

How to 'read' an element

The element title

The **element title** gives a broad description of what you must do. The verb (the 'doing' word) will show you the approach you need, e.g. investigate, examine, use, search and retrieve.

The performance criteria

The **performance criteria** say what activities must be completed. Your evidence will be matched against these performance criteria to check that your work is acceptable.

Element title

Element 3.1: Examine working with information technology

PERFORMANCE CRITERIA
A student must:

Performance criteria

1 indentify and give examples of **jobs** which involve working with information technology

2 identify and give examples of organisations that employ people to do these **jobs**

3 **compare ways** in which organisations prepare, process and present information

RANGE
Jobs: using IT, providing IT service, providing IT products

Range

Organisations: those using IT, IT suppliers

Compare: speed, ease of use, effort, accuracy

Ways: manual, automated

EVIDENCE INDICATORS
A list:

Evidence indicators

- identifying different types of jobs, covering the range and providing two examples of each type of job

- identifying different organisations that employ people to do these jobs, covering the range and providing two examples of each type of organisation.

A summary comparing the ways two different organisations prepare, process and present information.

AMPLIFICATION
Using IT (PC1 and PC2 range) for example processing documents, numerical data, graphics, databases, and control of production processes.
Providing IT services (PC1 and PC2 range) for example user support, system maintenance, hardware and software maintenance, servicing and repair, network management, database management.
Providing IT products (PC1 and PC2 range) for example IT systems design, software production, manufacturer, publishing.
Organisations using IT (PC2 range) for example shops, factories, banks, booking, agencies, offices.
IT suppliers (PC2 range) for example computer manufacturers, software producers, computer shops, IT maintenance and support agencies.
Prepare information (PC3) the way in which data may be collected, recorded (eg a mark in a box or with MICR), or presented on a data sheet where there are boxes for each character to enable the operator to enter it more easily.

Amplification

GUIDANCE
This element ensures that students' understanding of jobs which involve working with information technology is based on sound practical experience. Computer magazines and newspapers could be used to identify and classify jobs in information technology, and to compare ways in which computer organisations prepare and present advertising materials.

Guidance

Figure I.2 **Parts of Element 3.1**

The range

The **range** lists the skills, knowledge and understanding you will need to meet the performance criteria.

Evidence indicators

The **evidence indicators** tell you the *minimum* evidence that your portfolio should contain to achieve the award. More information about what to include in your portfolio is given below.

Amplification

The **amplification** section gives extra information. It may explain terms used in the performance criteria or the range, or explain what is *not* to be covered. It may also give examples.

Guidance

The **guidance** notes are written mainly for the teachers. This section offers suggestions about links between elements and gives ideas for teaching methods.

The portfolio

Use your portfolio to keep all the evidence collected as you work through the units. It must contain at least the minimum stated in the evidence indicators section of each element.

When marking your work, your teacher is looking for the right quality and quantity of work. He or she will first check that you have covered everything. They will also check the evidence indicators, and that you have covered *all* items in the range. However, work of a high quality may earn you a merit or distinction award, so your teacher will be looking at this too.

The evidence indicators use special terms – like list, notes, records and summary – to show what *depth* of work is needed, and you need to check that you have met this level of presentation.

Lists

Lists are simply a series of brief comments on the main points. Figure I.3(a) shows an example from Element 1.1.

Notes

Notes are more than just a list. For each item, you may write a paragraph of information. You may also write notes when preparing for a task. They may include draft ideas, initial plans and drawings, and so on. Figure I.3(b) shows an example from Element 3.3.

Observation of performance

Your teacher will watch you working, and then write an assessment of your performance. In some situations another person, e.g. your supervisor in a work placement, may observe you. Figure I.3(c) shows an example from Element 1.3.

Presentation

A presentation is more formal. You will present your finished work to an audience (maybe only to your teacher), but your evidence portfolio might include a taped recording or a video together with the material (e.g. OHPs or slides) that you used. Figure I.3(d) shows an example from Element 3.2.

Your teacher will be responsible for agreeing that you used a good standard of English during your presentation, and that your manner and tone were suitable for your audience.

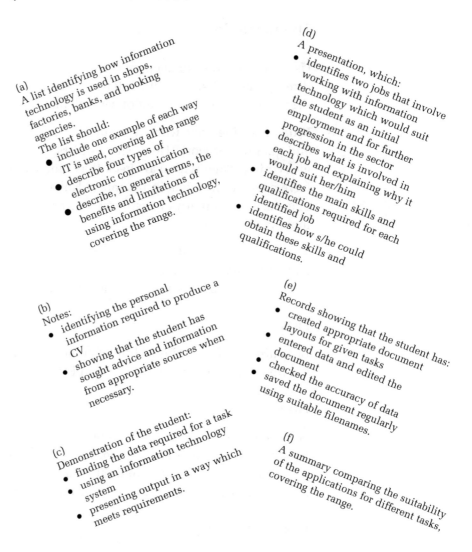

(a)
A list identifying how information technology is used in shops, factories, banks, and booking agencies.
The list should:
- include one example of each way IT is used, covering all the range
- describe four types of electronic communication
- describe, in general terms, the benefits and limitations of using information technology, covering the range.

(b)
Notes:
- identifying the personal information required to produce a CV
- showing that the student has sought advice and information from appropriate sources when necessary.

(c)
Demonstration of the student:
- finding the data required for a task
- using an information technology system
- presenting output in a way which meets requirements.

(d)
A presentation, which:
- identifies two jobs that involve working with information technology which would suit the student as an initial employment and for further progression in the sector
- describes what is involved in each job and explaining why it would suit her/him
- identifies the main skills and qualifications required for each identified job
- identifies how s/he could obtain these skills and qualifications.

(e)
Records showing that the student has:
- created appropriate document layouts for given tasks
- entered data and edited the document
- checked the accuracy of data saved the document regularly using suitable filenames.

(f)
A summary comparing the suitability of the applications for different tasks, covering the range.

Figure I.3 **Example evidence indicators**

Record

This is an account of the activity which is being assessed. It could be a written record, including tables of data, a check-list of activities, and so on. You can decide exactly what to include after discussion with your teacher. See Figure I.3(e) for an example from Element 2.1.

Report

A report is a finished piece of work which brings together lots of ideas and information. At foundation level no reports are expected as evidence of mandatory units. They will be required, however, for the optional units, e.g. Elements 5.2, 6.1, 8.1 and 9.1.

Summary

A summary is a *short* account similar to a record, but should not include all your working papers. Figure I.3(f) shows an example from Element 1.2.

Other evidence

Elements may ask for a special form of evidence to be produced by you. For example:

- Element 2.1 asks for two documents
- Element 2.2 asks for two graphics
- Elements 2.3 and 2.4 ask for computer output
- Element 3.3 asks for a copy of your CV

Grading

By the end of your course, your portfolio will contain a great deal of evidence.

In deciding what grade to award (pass, merit, or distinction) your teacher will consider:

- your approach to learning and how you tackled your work
- how much responsibility you took for planning your work
- how you decided what information you needed
- how well you reviewed and evaluated your own progress
- the quality of your evidence

It is important, therefore, to aim high.

During your course, you should receive feedback from your teacher which will give you a clear picture of how you are doing, and how you might improve your performance.

The grading criteria used by your teacher are grouped into the following four themes:

1. Planning
   - Drawing up plans of action
   - Monitoring courses of action
2. Information seeking and information handling
   - Identifying information needs
   - Identifying and using sources to obtain information
3. Evaluation
   - Evaluating outcomes and justifying approaches

4. Quality of outcomes
   - Synthesis
   - Command of language

Figure I.4 explains the difference between merit and distinction.

	Merit	Distinction
Theme 1: Planning *Drawing up plans for action* Student independently draws up plans which prioritise the different tasks within the given time period.	Plans cover a series of discrete tasks.	Plans cover complex activities.
Monitoring courses of action Student independently identifies points at which monitoring is necessary and recognises where revisions to courses of action are necessary. Appropriate revisions to plans are made.	Revisions to plans are made with guidance from teacher/tutor.	Revisions are made independently.
Theme 2: Information seeking and information handling *Identifying information needs* Student independently identifies the information requirements.	Information requirements relate to a series of discrete tasks.	Information requirements relate to complex activities.
Identifying and using sources to obtain information Student independently accesses and collects relevant information.	Information requirements relate to a series of discrete tasks. Student identifies principal sources independently and additional sources are identified by the teacher/tutor.	Information requirements relate to complex activities. Student uses a range of sources and justifies their selection.
Theme 3: Evaluation *Evaluating outcomes and justifying approaches* Student judges outcomes against original criteria for success.	Student justifies the approach used and indicates that alternatives were identified and considered.	Student justifies the approach used with a detailed consideration of relevant advantages and disadvantages. Alternatives and improvements are identified.
Theme 4: Quality of outcomes *Synthesis* Student's work demonstrates an effective synthesis of knowledge skills and understanding…	…in response to discrete tasks.	…in response to complex activities.
Command of 'language' Student's work demonstrates a command of the 'language' of the GNVQ area at foundation/intermediate level.	Student demonstrates an effective command.	Student demonstrates a fluent command.

Figure I.4 **Grading criteria and the difference between merit and distinction**

The external test

When you have completed the work for a single unit you should be ready to sit the external test.

These tests are set for all foundation mandatory units, but not the optional units. They are written tests, usually taking one hour, and all questions are multiple choice.

Which ONE of the following could be used to highlight an important word in a document?

a embolden
b copy
c move
d cut and paste

Figure I.5 **Sample multiple choice question**

Figure I.5 uses a **stem** which starts: 'Which ONE of the following...' Notice that the word 'ONE' is written in capitals. This is to help you, so read the stem carefully, and watch for these extra clues.

There are always four **choices**: a, b, c or d. These are written next to the four possible answers. Note that only one of them is correct – to earn a mark you must make the correct choice.

Another type of question – still multiple choice – is shown in Figure I.6. This time the stem is a sentence which needs to be completed. You must choose one of statements (a, b, c or d) to finish the sentence and make a true statement.

You will be given a special form to use during the examination. On this you mark which answer you think is the right one for each question.

Some tips

1. Read each question – the stem and all four 'answers' – very carefully.
2. Try to decide if any of the four choices is definitely wrong. This will narrow your choice down to two or three instead of four.

3. Think very carefully about the remaining choices.
4. If you still feel unsure and cannot decide, then make a 'best guess'. Do not waste a question by not giving an answer.

A tab would be useful when:

a underlining a heading
b inputting a table of figures
c using a keyboard
d using a mouse

Figure 1.6 **Sample multiple choice question**

How should you use this book?

This book is divided into three sections, which match the three mandatory units in Foundation GNVQ Information Technology.

- Section 1 covers the work of Unit 1: IT systems and their components.
- Section 2 covers the work of Unit 2: the use of IT for processing documents and graphics, modelling data and process control.
- Section 3 covers the work of Unit 3: the jobs available that involve working with IT.

Each section is then divided into chapters, and each chapter concentrates on one element of a unit. Included in each chapter there are:

- notes on what you need to know
- activities to test your understanding

At the end of each section, a sample test for that whole unit is given. At the end of the book, the correct answers to these tests are given.

What else do you need?

As well as this book, you need a copy of the unit specifications for Foundation GNVQ Information Technology.

The NCVQ (National Council for Vocational Qualifications) publishes a booklet which includes specifications for the following at level 1:

- mandatory and optional units for Foundation GNVQ Information Technology
- core skills units in:
  - Application of Number
  - Communication
  - Information Technology

This booklet explains the GNVQ course and is essential reading. Your school or college may supply copies of this booklet for reference purposes. You can purchase your own copy (£2.50 including postage) from:

NCVQ
222 Euston Road
London
NW1 2BZ

Telephone: 0171 728 1957

Acknowledgements

Thanks are due for the support received while writing this book:

- to all my colleagues at RSA – everyone in the GNVQ unit, and the team of setters, pre-moderators and moderators involved in the preparation of external test papers
- to my counterparts at BTEC and City & Guilds, and the staff at NVCQ
- to my family who often lost sight of me during the months of preparation of this book

I am grateful to all those who provided material for the many examples in the book:

- George Honour, Family Butcher, Old Woking
- Karen and Michael Hall, Cycleman, Ashford
- the Green Team staff at Chris Lane's, Old Woking, especially Alison O'Brien who supplied the graphics for many of the figures in this book
- Peter Wildgoose and his colleagues, London Taxis International, Coventry
- Peter Pitchforth, Midland Bank Pensioners' Association, for the poem on page 57
- Alex Guild, National Westminster Bank

The introduction of computerised systems into shops has affected both staff and customers. We look at the effect on staff in Chapter 8. Here, we will concentrate on the customers.

ACTIVITY 1.1

Next time you visit a shop, take note of the methods used for pricing goods.

- Does each item have a price sticker?
- Is a bar code system in use? (See page 10 for more details of bar coding.)
- What about items sold by weight? How are these priced?

Pricing

George Honour, the butcher, displays his prices in the shop window and has a complete **list of current prices** on display behind the counter. Prices may change daily and George Honour, his staff and the customers need a list to refer to.

Customers usually ask for meat by quantity: half a pound of sausages, three chicken quarters or a piece of beef. The item is weighed on electronic scales and a price displayed automatically as soon as the price per pound is entered.

Karen Hall puts **price labels** on all her stock items – which takes a lot of time – but it means her customers can see the price of every item before deciding to buy. Karen's shop offers a lot of choice, and often the price will be an important factor.

Some shops, especially clothes shops, use **Kimball tags**: small cards punched with holes to identify the item (Figure 1.1). This tag is detached when the item is sold and collected by the shop assistant for later processing. The Kimball tag cards are read automatically by machine and are used to update the stock files.

In the bar at Chris Lane's, a **list of prices** is on display; this is a legal requirement for all licensed premises. Members ask for drinks by the measure: half a pint of lager, a pint of Guinness or a gin and tonic. The bar staff use a **concept keyboard** to tap in the drinks ordered. The till displays the name of the drink and its price, and automatically calculates the total amount due.

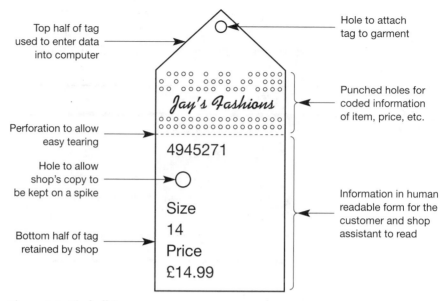

Figure 1.1 **Kimball tag**

Supermarkets with point-of-sale (POS) systems rely on **bar codes** at the check-out. These codes are printed on the product packaging or label and read by a machine. Prices are only displayed on a shelf label.

Items that are sold by weight are handled in one of two ways:

1. The assistant bags up the required amount, weighs it and sticks on a label showing the price. At the check-out, the assistant keys in this amount.

2. The shopper or the assistant bags up the required amount and the check-out assistant places it on an automatic scale, keys in a product code and the price is calculated automatically.

Having no price stickers on each item is a possible disadvantage for shoppers. It is easy to fill a trolley and yet have no real idea of how much it will cost altogether. To overcome this some supermarkets now provide trolleys with calculators.

Working out the bill

ACTIVITY 1.2

Next time you visit a shop, take note of how the cashier works out the total bill.

- Do they calculate the total due and handwrite a receipt for you?
- Do they use a bar code scanner to register your purchase?
- Does the till produce an itemised receipt?

George Honour and his staff make a note of the price of each item bought by their customers on a notepad (Figure 1.2).

Figure 1.2 **Example notepad sheet**

When all items have been bagged up, they calculate the total mentally. As a check, the assistant adds it up again. Many customers have their meat order delivered and for them a handwritten bill is produced (Figure 1.3).

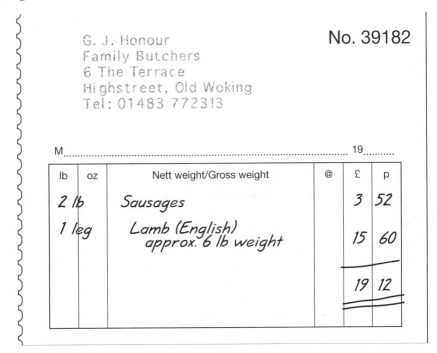

Figure 1.3 **Handwritten bill**

George says he usually adds up these bills using a calculator – but just to be sure, he then double-checks the calculations in his head!

Mark Foster's till adds up the total amount due for a round of drinks but no receipt is printed for the customer.

Karen Hall uses a till to enter each item's price separately. The till roll has two copies: one is torn off and given to the customer as a receipt, the other remains in the till as a printed record of all transactions for that day. The customer's receipt does not give any information about the products purchased.

A point-of-sale (POS) system refers to a computer database to find out details of each product purchased. This system uses the bar code as a key. The receipts show an itemised list of the purchases made, which can be very helpful to the shopper.

Making payment

Using cash for payment increases risks for both the customer and the shopkeeper:

- The customer has to carry large sums of cash – enough to pay bills – and runs the risk of losing it or being robbed.
- The shopkeeper has to keep sufficient change in the till (although, legally, it is the responsibility of the shopper to have the right money).
- The shopkeeper has to bank large amounts of cash and runs the risk of being robbed, either at the shop or on the way to the bank.

Both customers and shopkeepers find it more convenient to use one or more of the alternative payment methods (Figure 1.4). It also usually saves time.

ACTIVITY 1.3

Next time you visit a shop, find out how many different methods of payment are available to you. Does the shop accept payment:

- by cash?
- by cheque?
- by credit card?
- by debit card?
- by store card?

Figure 1.4 **Shop window signs showing payment methods accepted**

Mark Foster expects all customers to pay by cash but George Honour accepts cheques (with a cheque guarantee card). Karen and Michael Hall's shop sells items which often exceed the amount guaranteed on a cheque card, so she accepts credit cards such as Access or Visa. Shops like the large supermarket chains will also accept debit cards, such as Switch and Delta (Figure 1.5).

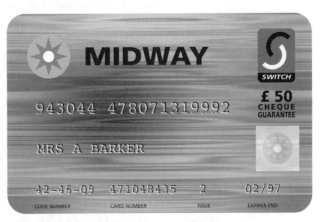

Figure 1.5 **'Switch' debit card**

IT has dramatically changed the way people pay for goods. More details about cheques and credit/debit/store cards are given later in this chapter, in the section on banking (page 23).

Shopping is also possible without even visiting shops. You can telephone a supplier, place an order and arrange to pay by credit card. This service is commonly used for florists, booking agencies (which we also look at in more detail later in this chapter) and mail order.

IT has also had an effect on other aspects of retailing. It is used in shops for many things, such as:

- automated billing using bar codes
- stock control
- payroll

Automated billing using bar codes

The assistants in some small shops, like George Honour's butcher shop and most street traders, calculate your total bill, either in their head or by writing amounts down as your goods are packed. Probably you will pay by cash.

For shops, like Karen and Michael Hall's cycle shop, with many product lines there are too many products for the shop assistant to remember all the prices, so sticky price labels are put on each item. Then the assistant reads this and keys the amount into the till. The receipt just shows a list of prices, and the total amount to pay.

Nowadays, most food items have a bar code stamped on the tin or packet, and many shops use bar codes to identify products at the cash desk. This provides several benefits:

1. There is no risk of the cashier entering the wrong price, so it is more accurate.
2. It is a quick alternative to a cashier entering the price directly through a keypad. This means customers can expect to be served more quickly.
3. The system can produce an itemised bill which gives extra information to the shopper.
4. The store can change a price (up or down!) by altering the price held on the IT system. There is no need to price goods individually, or to re-price goods when there is a price change. This saves a lot of time and means the shop can reduce the number of staff employed – or use them for other duties such as helping shoppers to pack their goods or collecting trolleys.

5. It is possible to link the bar code system to a stock control system. The shop then has tighter control over stock and should be able to re-order items before they run out.

How do bar code systems work?

A bar code is a pattern of black and white lines (Figure 1.6). The pattern represents a code number, and can be read automatically by a scanning device. The code does not include the price – which might change – but is used to look up the price held on a central computer. Because the bar code scanner records that an item has been sold these systems also allows automatic updating of stock records. Automatic stock records then allow automatic re-ordering of goods.

Figure 1.6 **Bar code**

Stock control

Stock control includes:

- keeping track of incoming stock
- keeping track of sales
- noticing when stock levels are low
- re-ordering stock in time

Shops selling many thousands of product lines would find it very difficult to control their stock without using computerised stock control systems.

Stock records used to be kept on paper, or most probably cards, in the storeroom. In a small supermarket the manager would decide how much to order by looking around the storeroom and consulting these stock record cards.

In deciding the quantity to order, two things are important:

1. the rate of sales of an item
2. how long it might be before delivery would be made

If the manager made a mistake, and ordered too little, the shop could run out of an item and customers might have been disappointed. If this were to happen too often, customers might decide to use a different shop altogether.

If the manager ordered too much, it could be an expensive mistake. Goods might pass their sell-by date, or just go out of fashion before they could be sold.

Having more stock than you really need ties up capital. There may also be a storage problem!

'Where do you want this one, guv?'

Using a computerised stock control system means the store manager can order as little stock as possible (reducing stock overheads to a minimum) but order it soon enough to avoid running out of any product line, and still have room to move around in the storeroom.

This does not mean that supermarkets *never* run out of stock items! Customers may buy far more than usual, for instance if a particular item appears on a cookery programme and is essential for a recipe. Suppliers may also fail to deliver on time and cause problems for the shop.

It should also be noted that if stock is stolen (or broken or otherwise made unsaleable) the IT system may show a higher stock level than is actually on the shelves. Regular physical stock checks are therefore still necessary to ensure that the IT system is basing re-ordering decisions on accurate data.

'According to the computer there are plenty in stock.'

Payroll

Shops employ many people to fill the shelves, serve customers, collect trolleys, clean the store, etc.

Many of these staff work part-time and irregular hours. They may also be paid productivity bonuses. Calculating the wages of staff is an important task. It has to be done as quickly as possible and accurately.

Shops with many staff may therefore choose to use a payroll package to process the wages automatically.

Data collection

Each pay period (a week or a month), information would be collected about what hours each employee had worked. Some shops might use time cards that are punched when employees arrive and leave. Other shops may expect section supervisors to keep written records and to present a summary to the payroll staff for processing.

Clocking in

The information needed to calculate a payroll falls into three types: static information, past history data and current data.

- **Static information** about the employee – e.g. name, address, department code, tax code, National Insurance (NI) number – rarely changes, unless a person moves house or gets married.
- **Past history** – e.g. pay to date, tax paid to date – must be amended each period to keep it up-to-date.
- **Current data** includes hours worked this period.

Data processing

For each new period the current data will be inputed. This is used to calculate that period's pay and to update past history data.

Reports

At the year end (the tax year ends in April, not December) all employers have to present information to the Inland Revenue

(Figure 1.7). If the payroll is computerised, these year-end reports can be produced automatically.

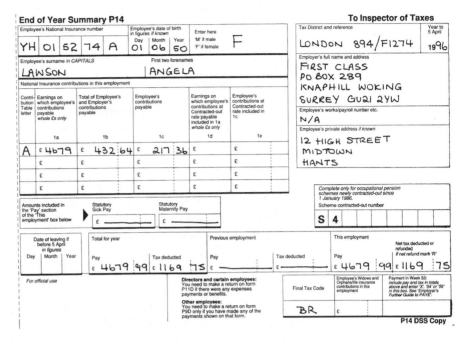

Figure 1.7 **Sample P14 – an end of year summary of an employee's pay**

The benefits of using IT for payroll calculations

Payroll was one of the first applications to be computerised because it proved to be ideal for computing:

- different data for each employee, e.g. hours worked and rates of pay
- complicated extras like overtime and holiday pay
- complicated calculations based on tax codes, rates and bands
- high volumes of data to be processed in a short space of time
- the need for accuracy of calculations and reliable information storage

As a bonus, a computerised system also provides year-end data – this can save a lot of time for the accounts department of any company.

To date, no disadvantages have been identified! Can you think of any?

Factories

Factories buy raw materials and components and, from these, produce an end product. Their customers may be large companies who buy direct from the factory, or retailers who will sell the product through their shops.

Information technology is used in factories for many things, such as:

- automated production
- goods ordering
- invoicing
- stock control
- payroll

Automated production methods

Automation is the use of machines (e.g. conveyor belts, robots, computers) to do tasks previously performed by people.

CAD/CAM (computer-aided design/computer-aided manufacture) is the use of the results of a CAD process (as input) to control a CAM process. This can be an integrated process in which the manufacturing happens automatically and is often important in the development of new products.

CNC (computer numeric control) is the automatic control of machines such as lathes and milling machines. Some machines simply obey a program of instructions; others perform more advanced tasks involving sensors and feedback systems.

ACTIVITY 1.4

Find out how a car wash works. How many different programmes are offered? How does the machinery 'know' what to do? Are sensors used in the process?

Cybernetics is the study of the control of processes by a computer, e.g. an industrial process or a robot.

Robotics is the study and design of robots. A robot is a computer-controlled mechanical device. It has to be flexible enough to do a variety of tasks. Frequently, robots are used for jobs where consistent performance is required (e.g. paint-spraying motor cars) or where there would be some danger to humans performing the task (e.g. handling toxic materials or defusing a bomb). A **robot arm** is a relatively simple fixed robot capable of manipulating items by picking them up, moving them to another position, etc. (Figure 1.8).

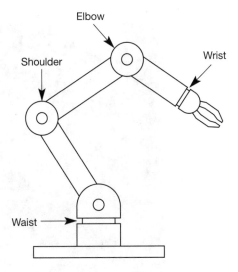

Figure 1.8 **Robot arm**

IT systems are often used to automate industrial production, particularly work which was previously done manually and was labour-intensive or dangerous. Examples are:

- paint-spraying objects using spray guns
- moving cars down a production line on automated transport units
- computer-controlled metal shaping performed by mills and lathes
- handling radioactive materials

CASE STUDY

London Taxis International

London Taxis International (LTI) produce the distinctive London taxi – or black cab.

LTI use the latest **CAD technology** to design a chassis to the highest standards – of comfort, safety, security and value for money.

Wide doors, a flat floor, a spacious interior, easily located ramps and an electronic locking mechanism are essential design features making the taxi accessible for wheelchair users. LTI aim to meet the needs of all passengers, including those with small children, pushchairs and luggage, making their ride as comfortable and safe as possible.

LTI also use robotics in their factory, to cut pieces of metal ready for assembly.

Plasma cutter at ITC working on a cab section

The metal is loaded onto a carriage, and slid automatically into position for cutting. The plasma cutter is pre-programmed to follow a route. It senses the position of the metal, and the cutting arm can move in all three directions to achieve the desired result. When the cutting process has finished the piece is moved beyond the cutter, leaving room for the next piece. This cutting process can also be achieved by workers manually feeding the piece of metal into a machine, making the necessary movements with their arms to guide the piece through. These workers are highly skilled with many years of training; to learn how to cut a new shape would take them a long time. To retrain the robot is much easier.

Goods ordering

Factories use raw materials and components to make end products. Usually, each end product needs many different parts.

Karen and Michael Hall receive the parts for bikes from their suppliers and have to build the bikes before they can be sold to their customers. Their bikes arrive with all the necessary parts, so their job is made easier.

ACTIVITY 1.5

Imagine how many different parts a car manufacturer has to have available before a car can be built. Make a list of six major components of a car. Choose one major component (e.g. a wheel) and list what components are needed to make that single component.

It is important that the factory does not run out of stock of any of the parts needed. If they do, it may lead to closure of a production line and delay in production. Workers may have nothing to do while they wait for parts to arrive. Orders may not be completed on time. Customers may decide to order the products from a more reliable supplier.

A factory may have only a few regular suppliers and order the same items almost every time. They may produce an order for goods using a word processor by amending the quantities requested on a previous order.

Some factories have a communications link with their supplier and place orders directly using a computer terminal. This kind of link is used by organisations who need supplies very quickly and yet have little notice of their requirements. A good example is a car repair centre. They do not know what parts will be needed for any repair job until the damaged vehicle arrives – and then they need to have all the parts straight away, because the customer expects a very quick service.

'It needs the lot!'

Invoicing

An invoice is a document which records goods or services supplied to a customer and requests payment (see Figure 1.9). The invoice is prepared by the supplier of the goods or services and sent to the customer. Sometimes the invoice is with the goods; sometimes the invoice will be sent at a later date.

Most companies prepare invoices on a regular basis – daily, weekly or monthly – depending on what they are selling. A small company may send out only ten invoices a day; a large company, like gas or electricity suppliers, may send out thousands every day. Preparing these invoices and keeping track of which customers have paid their invoices – or more importantly, which ones have not paid – is essential.

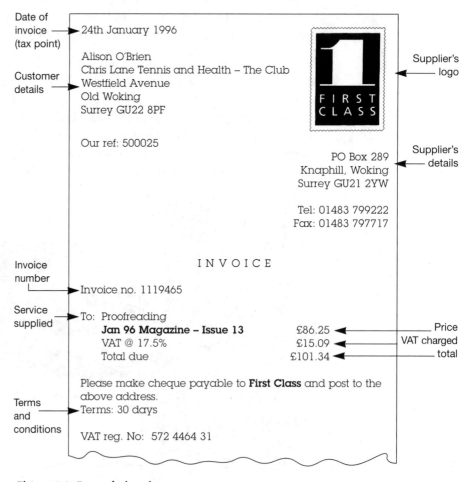

Figure 1.9 **Example invoice**

Invoices are legal documents and have to contain certain details:

- who is the supplier of the goods
- what goods were supplied
- who is the receiver of the goods
- the value of the goods
- the date (called the tax point) of the invoice

In the UK, a tax is charged on all sales. This is called VAT (value added tax) and currently stands at $17\frac{1}{2}$ per cent on most goods. All companies have to keep track of the value of their invoices and the amount of VAT charged to their customers. They also keep track of invoices received from their suppliers and VAT charged on those invoices. The difference in the VAT amounts has to be paid to Customs and Excise regularly. In this way, the government charges a tax on the difference between what it costs to buy supplies and what the company earns from selling the finished products.

Invoicing is one of the most popular IT applications. It uses three main sources of information:

1. **Customer details** – company name, address, special terms such as discounts allowed.
2. **Product details** – product code, product description, price.
3. **Order details** – what goods have been ordered by each customer.

From this data, an invoice is created which involves a calculation to arrive at a total amount due.

Once the two databases have been set up – one for products and one for customers – production of invoices becomes an easy task.

Benefits of using IT for invoicing

Invoicing uses the same data over and over again, e.g. a customer's name and address, the product code and description. Having this data on an IT system means that:

- The data is only keyed once (hopefully correctly).
- The data can be revised and printed out in many forms, such as on an invoice, on a statement chasing up payment or on a letter threatening legal action if payment is not received.

Invoicing requires complex calculations, such as:

- multiplying the quantity ordered by the price
- adding up the cost of all products ordered
- calculating any discounts or taxes such as VAT

This can be done quickly and accurately on an IT system.

As a by-product of invoicing, the factory may also obtain reports about which customers have not paid their invoices, and how much is owed to the company.

Stock control

Factories keep records of how much stock is held in their stores but this may be more complicated than systems used by shops. This is because a factory uses raw materials which may be supplied in bulk but are used a little at a time.

A production line may need many different items (or 'parts') all of which must be in stock if the end product is to be produced on time and the line kept fully operational.

Payroll

Like shops, factories may employ many people. They may be **salaried**, earning the same amount each month regardless of the hours worked, or on a **wage**, based on an hourly rate and the actual hours worked.

Wage earners tend to clock in and out of factories and their pay is calculated from this data.

At London Taxis International all employees clock in to a computerised system. This allows the supervisors in charge of each production line to see if they have enough staff to run the line, and to make quick decisions if employees need to be moved from one production line to another.

It is also possible to link a computerised clocking-in system to a payroll system.

Banks

Banks provide shops, factories, companies and customers with the facility to pay, or be paid, for services or products. To use the services of a bank, a customer can open an **account** with one or more of the many banks. Several different types of account are available, such as:

- saving or deposit accounts
- cheque accounts

Saving accounts are used to deposit money – often quite large sums – and to earn interest on the balance in the account. A **cheque account** gives the bank customer the option to write cheques in payment for goods bought. With this type of account the bank usually provides a bank guarantee card. This allows the bank customer to write cheques (up to a certain limit) and to guarantee that the bank will honour the cheque (even if there is not enough money in the account).

The bank may also supply a **cash card** which allows the bank customer to make withdrawals from an ATM (automated teller machine), otherwise known as 'the hole in the wall'.

ACTIVITY 1.6

Visit an ATM with a friend or member of your family who has a cash card. Notice what steps they take to draw out cash (but do not try to see their PIN number!). Write down the sequence of steps needed to access the machine. What other services are offered at the ATM?

An ATM or 'hole in the wall'

For businesses, banks charge a fee (usually based on the amount of money passing through the account) in return for which they supply a number of 'extra' services, such as:

- advice on setting up a business
- leaflets on how to calculate cash flow
- loans or overdraft facilities
- transfer options, e.g. BACS (see page 25) for swift and easy payment of staff and suppliers

Banks have many thousands of customers, each making many transactions every day – paying money in, writing cheques and so on. It is important for all calculations to be accurate and for information to be up-to-date.

IT is therefore used in banks for many things, including:

- keeping customer account records
- transferring money between accounts

Transfer of money between two bank accounts is possible in many ways, for instance:

- by cheque
- by electronic funds transfer (EFT)
- by standing order
- by direct debit

Electronic funds transfer (EFT)

Instead of using paper (bank notes, cheques, or banker's drafts) money can be transferred electronically, using EFT.

EFT uses the computer networks to transfer money between banks. It is especially useful where international transfers are involved. The same principles are involved when you withdraw cash from the cash dispenser of an automatic teller machine (ATM).

Increasingly, **debit cards**, e.g. Switch cards (see Figure 1.5, page 9), are being accepted in retail stores as an alternative to payment by credit card or cheque. The customer offers a debit card which is processed in the same way as a credit card, but the money is transferred from the purchaser's account directly to the shop's account. This is known as **electronic funds transfer at point-of-sale** (EFTPOS).

Direct debit

The term 'direct debit' is often confused with 'debit' cards, but they are very different. Direct debits are similar to standing orders but differ in one important way.

Bank account holders can instruct their own bank to pay money from their account to another account by setting up a **standing order**. Usually, this will be for a fixed amount on a regular basis, e.g. £25 each month to British Gas, or a mortgage payment to a building society.

Alternatively, the bank account holder may authorise their bank to accept a **direct debit** request from another bank. For example, you can now pay your telephone bill by direct debit. British Telecom informs your bank of the amount of the bill and take that amount from your account. The amount taken may (and most probably will) vary.

Direct debit appears less safe – because the account holder has authorised for *any* amount to be taken – but there are safeguards which should protect account holders.

Bankers automated clearing services (BACS)

BACS is the banking service which allows direct payment from one account to many others. It may be used to pay wages into employee accounts or to pay invoices into supplier's accounts. Most large companies now pay their employees and their suppliers by BACS.

Payroll

Like shops and factories, banks have many employees and use a payroll system to pay their staff.

ACTIVITY 1.7

Try to remember all the reasons why a payroll is computerised. Obtain a copy of a payslip and identify which items are calculated automatically by the computer.

Booking agencies

Booking agencies offer a service (booking a place for you). It may be for:

- travel – a plane flight, or a hire car
- accommodation – an overnight stay in a hotel, or a fortnight's stay in a villa
- entertainment – tickets for a show, or an important sports event

The booking agency is linked by computer network to the providers of these services: travel companies, hotels or theatres, and so on.

Travel

Within the UK, you can travel by air, rail, coach or bus – as well as by private transport. For air, rail and coach services it is usually necessary to book in advance, to reserve your seat and guarantee your place on that plane, train or coach. Airports, main-line stations and coach stations operate the booking system.

When booking air travel, you can choose between different levels of service: first class, business or economy. You can also make special requests, e.g. for vegetarian food or extra leg-room.

The airlines have many routes, many planes on these routes and many passengers on each plane. If the booking system was not computerised, it would be impossible to keep track.

The main benefit for the traveller is the speed at which availability of flights can be found out, and confirmation of a booking made.

The airlines aim to fill their flights – usually by selling spare seats at reduced prices – and to maximise their profits.

Accommodation

Nowadays, most large hotels use a computerised booking system to record all room bookings. Cleaning rotas can be established using information about expected departures; vacated rooms are cleaned first so they are ready for that day's arrivals. On arrival, a guest can then be allocated their room immediately.

The booking system can also record any purchases made during the guest's visit, e.g. use of telephone, restaurant bills or laundry service. The guest's bill can then be produced automatically on the morning of departure.

Entertainment

Theatres need full houses for every show if they are to maximise profits. Shows are advertised and critics review the performances of the actors taking part. This creates interest by the public. For the most popular shows you have to book a long time in advance. For less popular shows you could turn up on the night and hope to get a seat.

To maximise the sale of seats, most theatres use booking agencies. The booking agency may be in a hotel, at a large railway station or at an airport. People then do not need to visit the theatre to book tickets in advance.

Telephone bookings are also possible. In this case the purchase usually involves paying by credit card.

Types of electronic communication

From the earliest cave drawings, man has used many ways to communicate.

The three main methods used to communicate are:

- by **sound** – jungle drums, car horn
- by **light** – a lighthouse signal or a heliograph
- by **electronic means**

ACTIVITY 1.8

Find out what a heliograph is. Write short notes to explain how it works.

Messages sent by sound are slow compared with those sent by light waves. Sound travels at 760 m.p.h. while light travels at 670 million m.p.h! This is why thunder is heard after lightning flashes – a delay of 5 seconds per mile.

Light messages travel quickly but both sender and receiver must be in sight of one another.

Electricity was first used to transmit messages by **needle telegraph**; you will have heard of **Morse code**.

In 1861, the first **telephone** was demonstrated in Germany; the first British telephone exchange (in 1879) led to rapid growth in this direct form of spoken communication. Recently the telephone system has been extended, with the introduction of fax machines, to allow transmission of visual information such as documents and drawings.

In 1894, **radio** waves were used to send signals without wires – hence the term 'wireless'. **Television** appeared in 1926, allowing transmission of pictures as well as sounds. Nowadays, **satellites** allow these signals to travel further afield. These use **microwaves**, a form of high-frequency radio waves which allow for clearer signals.

ACTIVITY 1.9

Give three more examples of methods of communicating by sound or light – *not* electronically.

Television

Television allows communication of information in the form of moving pictures and sound.

A **camera** records a series of images (including the sound). This data is converted into electrical impulses and transmitted by radio to a receiver which then converts them using a cathode ray tube into an image on a screen (Figure 1.10).

Radio

This involves the transmission and reception of data using electro-magnetic waves at a frequency between 10^4 Hz and 3×10^{12} Hz, either as acoustic signals (called **radiotelephony**) or as Morse code signals (**radiotelegraphy**).

Telemetry uses communications (usually radio) and measuring sensors as part of a system for controlling machines and instruments at a distance, e.g. satellites and space probes. In Formula 1 racing it is used to monitor and control the performance of cars; the technicians can adjust the engine control system from the pits while the race is in progress.

Teletext

Teletext is a system that uses part of the broadcast TV picture, otherwise unseen to the viewer, to supply a variety of information, such as news items, weather forecasts, travel information and so on.

All TV channels in the UK offer this service; the BBC version is known as **Ceefax**. The commercial channels were originally known as **Oracle** until the name 'Teletext' was adopted as a brand name.

Viewers with a specially equipped TV set can replace the TV picture by text pages, simply by pressing buttons on a remote control handset.

Each page of information is numbered and all pages are transmitted in numerical sequence. A particular choice of page is made by entering

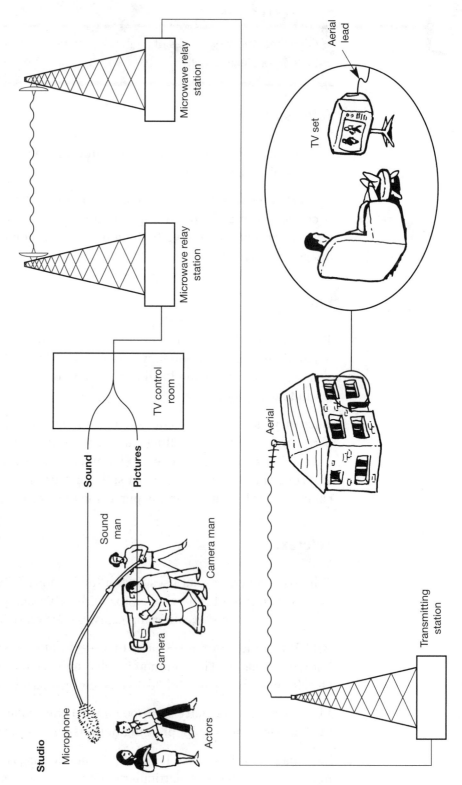

Figure 1.10 **How television pictures are created, transmitted and received**

the page number. There is a slight delay (until that page is next transmitted) before it appears on the screen.

The viewer cannot talk back to the provider of the pages of information, since this is only a one-way information service. Also, the waiting time limits the number of pages that can realistically be provided.

However, some pages are linked; 'Speedtext' – using coloured buttons – allows viewers to pass from one page to another more rapidly.

The Internet and the 'World Wide Web' now offer the user an almost unlimited amount of information. Like the teletext system, it displays 'pages' of textual and graphical information (Figure 1.11), either on a TV screen (linked to a 'set-top' computer) or, more generally, on a user's personal computer. Unlike teletext it uses regular telephone lines, rather than a broadcast TV signal, to transmit the information. This makes it possible for the user to interact with the system, for instance by requesting searches of valuable information, supplying information for other users to access, and ordering goods and services by credit card. Only those pages requested are transmitted, so (unlike teletext) very large amounts of data are accessible, with no penalty to other users of the system.

Figure 1.11 Web page

Telephone

Imagine calling a friend on the telephone. When you speak into the telephone receiver your voice causes vibrations which are converted into an electric current. This passes along a wire to your friend at the other end of the telephone line. It is then converted back into audible sound for your friend to hear. Their reply is sent back to you in the same way.

Facsimile (fax)

Fax transmission uses regular voice-quality telephone lines to send copies of documents, which may include drawings as well as text.

A **fax machine** (Figure 1.12), plugged into a telephone socket, allows you to transmit and receive copies of paper document pages. To send a fax, you first dial up the receiving machine, which must be available at that time (i.e. not busy sending or receiving another fax). When you hear the continuous tone, you press the 'start' button. Your fax machine then scans the paper on a line-by-line basis. This information

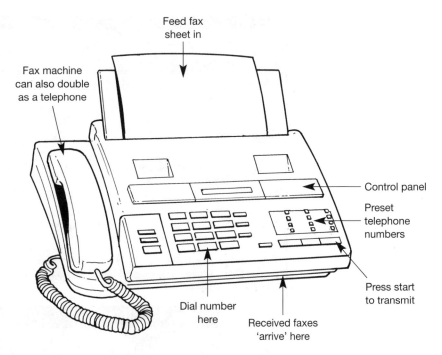

Figure 1.12 **Fax machine**

is transmitted along the telephone line to the receiving machine which recreates the document using photocopier technology. For this reason many fax machines can also operate as photocopiers.

The two fax machines must be compatible, i.e. belong to compatible groups, if they are to communicate. There are many different makes of fax machine, so to simplify the process of identifying compatibility, fax machines are classified into groups with different technical specifications.

If your computer is connected to the telephone line, you can send faxes directly without the need to generate a paper copy first. This solves the problem of the receiving machine being busy; your computer can simply try again later, without human intervention.

Electronic mail (e-mail)

E-mail messages are sent from user to user on a computer network, with the message being stored in the recipient's **mailbox** or **inbox** (Figure 1.13). The next time that they use the computer, they will be told that there is a message waiting, and can read it, print it out or reply.

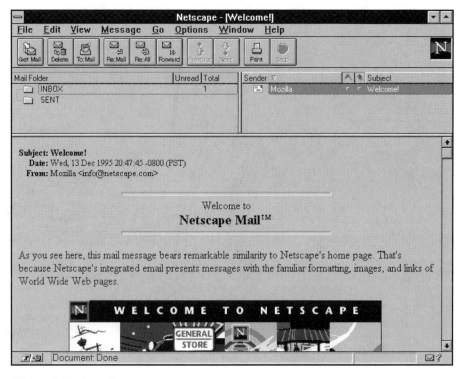

Figure 1.13 **E-mail screen**

Because e-mail is relatively cheap, and because the sender and the recipient do not both have to be using their computers at the same time, it is becoming a popular way for people in schools, colleges and in business to communicate.

Computer networks

There is also international co-operation between the larger networks, which allows messages to be sent internationally through 'gateways' between networks. The term '**Internet**' is used to describe this super-network. The principal academic network used for e-mail between British universities and colleges is **JANET** (Joint Academic Network).

ACTIVITY 1.10

Choose four different forms of electronic communication; write brief notes describing each of them.

Benefits

IT has provided many benefits for those using it – the shops, factories, banks, booking agencies and others – as well as their customers.

Speed

Computers can process data much faster than humans. Vast quantities of data can be stored and then accessed very quickly.

Computers save time because, for example, a word processing operator can make corrections to a stored version of a document, rather than having to re-key it.

ACTIVITY 1.11

Give three examples where computers have replaced humans to save time.

Cost

Although the cost of implementing IT can be very high, in the long run companies see cost savings. Many of these tend to be by replacing humans with computers.

ACTIVITY 1.12

Give three examples where computers have been installed to save money.

Accuracy

Humans easily make mistakes, for instance when adding up numbers. Working long hours can make people more tired, and they become even more prone to error.

Computers do not grow tired – they can be used for long periods, and their calculations will always provide accurate results.

ACTIVITY 1.13

Give three examples where accuracy is the most important reason for using a computer.

Impact on environment

In recent years, the importance of considering the effect on the environment has grown. Organisations like Greenpeace have brought many issues to the public eye by their sometimes daring activities. Using IT can have long-term effects on the users and the environment; and we can all make decisions that ensure these effects are not harmful. We now look at three topics and their possible impact on the environment.

Reduced need to travel

With more and more people working from home, the number of commuters has fallen. This reduces the number of car journeys taken and consequently reduces pollution of the atmosphere.

Similarly, the introduction of video conferencing facilities has made it easier for colleagues to 'meet' to discuss ideas without travelling.

Video conference v. night in the pub

ACTIVITY 1.14

What are the advantages of the reduced need to travel? What are the advantages of having more people working from home?

Monitoring and control systems

These enable early warning to be given of environmental pollution. Control systems used in energy conservation (e.g. heating systems) also help to reduce waste.

ACTIVITY 1.15

Look through newspaper reports to find three examples of monitoring and control systems which have a positive effect on the environment.

Social costs

There is no doubt that the industrial age resulted in men being replaced by machines. In the computer age men (and women) have again been replaced.

ACTIVITY 1.16

Give three examples of where people have lost jobs due to the introduction of computers. Have any jobs been created?

Nowadays, more people are working from home. For some, this is a better way of working.

ACTIVITY 1.17

Refer back to your list of the advantages of having more people working from home. Are there any disadvantages?

Limitations

However, IT can cause problems!

Security

Having data on an IT system rather than on paper means:

- lots of data can be stored on a single floppy disk
- the data is more easily moved and removed (and therefore stolen)
- if linked via networks, access can be quite easy

To improve security, we use two types of control:

1. physical control
2. logical control

Physical control includes locking doors, storing data in safes and issuing ID cards to users. **Logical control** includes using a password system and setting different access levels for different members of staff.

Problems

Sometimes, we hear horror stories. Instead of saying 'the cheque's in the post' the most popular excuse has become 'my computer has gone down.'

Errors

Errors can happen when:

- the operator makes a mistake while keying data
- the wrong disk or tape is used
- the hardware malfunctions
- the power fails

Equipment faults

Equipment faults can happen:

- with the hardware, e.g. the screen
- with the medium, e.g. the disk or tape

Loss of information

Loss of information can be damaging for the user. They can be embarrassed and might lose customers. At worst, a business might fail.

Health and safety considerations

The *Health and Safety at Work Act* (1974) dictates many aspects of working environments.

User

The user, i.e. the operator, must be protected from potential danger. Their seating is very important. Poor seating can result in poor posture and can cause back problems, and many more working hours are lost due to illnesses such as RSI (repetitive strain injury). RSI is a painful complaint which can make continuing work impossible. Usually it attacks the wrist or arm of people who have used a keyboard or mouse for a long time.

Ergonomics studies the relationship between people and their environment. Figure 1.14 shows the many different things that can be adjusted to make the operator as comfortable as possible:

- seat height
- table height
- keyboard position
- screen position

Figure 1.14 **Seating is important**

Equipment

Most computers are powered by mains electricity, and there are risks from the following:

- tripping over cables
- static electricity build up
- screen glare

ACTIVITY 1.18

Look at the cartoon of a 'nightmare office'. List all the dangers you can spot.

The nightmare office

Information

The type of information kept on an IT system (and possibly transmitted to other users) is subject to laws, for instance the control of pornography. Unfortunately, computers make the spread of this information easier and detection quite difficult. Also, information may be sensitive, e.g. medical records or financial details. If hackers gain access to computer files through a network, confidentiality may be lost.

New laws have been introduced to try to combat computer-based crime.

ACTIVITY 1.19

What laws have been introduced in the last 20 years which try to control information kept on an IT system?

Impact on the environment

It was expected that the introduction of computers would result in a paperless office. This eventually would cut down the amount of paper used and save the rainforests. Instead we use more paper, and create yet more waste with toner cartridges, old computer equipment and so on.

Recycling has become an important industry.

ACTIVITY 1.20

Find out what local facilities exist for recycling. Find out how local firms dispose of their paper waste. Can you think of any better alternatives?

The evidence indicators

To prove you have covered the material of this element you need to produce a list identifying how IT is used in shops, factories, banks and booking agencies.

The list should:

- include one example of each way IT is used
- describe four types of electronic communication
- describe, in general terms, the benefits and limitations of using IT

The material you have collected during the activities should provide enough evidence for this element. However, you can affect the grade you achieve by making sure your work is well presented. Look back over your work and try to improve it. Discuss with your teacher what needs to be done.

2 Describe common applications of information technology

This chapter covers the material needed for Element 1.2: Describe common applications of information technology.

The performance criteria state that the student must:

1. Identify and give examples of **common applications of information technology** used in offices.
2. Compare the suitability of common applications for different **tasks.**
3. Describe the **benefits and limitations of using common applications**.

Much of the theory covered in this chapter is important for the practical work that you will do in Unit 2.

The knowledge range

To meet the performance criteria, you *must* cover the range. The words shown in bold in the performance criteria above highlight the skills and knowledge you will need, and so we will consider each of these in turn.

Common applications of information technology

There are five common applications of IT:

1. word processing
2. desktop publishing (DTP)
3. databases
4. spreadsheets
5. graphics

Word processing

Word processing packages allow you to produce documents. The term 'word processing' is used to describe many things:

- text **editing** – entering and editing text
- text **formatting** – laying out a page, e.g. into columns
- producing printed **output**, including additional information

If the additional material includes graphics, we refer to **document processing** rather than word processing. If the additional material comes from a database, we call this a **mail merge**.

ACTIVITY 2.1

A word processing package is useful for producing letters. Think of four organisations which have high levels of correspondence and would use a word processor. Think of four other types of documents that these organisations might produce on a word processor.

Desktop publishing (DTP)

Desktop publishing is similar to document processing in that you can:

- enter and edit text
- incorporate images
- format the text

However, DTP provides more sophisticated facilities for **page make-up** which allow you to prepare material such as magazines, books or printed leaflets.

ACTIVITY 2.2

Think of three different organisations which might use DTP and suggest what kinds of documents they would produce.

Databases

A database is a computerised collection of information (data). IT systems can be used to store enormous amounts of data, but for this data to be useful it must be organised. This usually means grouping data items into **records** and then keeping the records in an order.

For example, the telephone directory gives an alphabetic list (sorted by surname) of data on each telephone number.

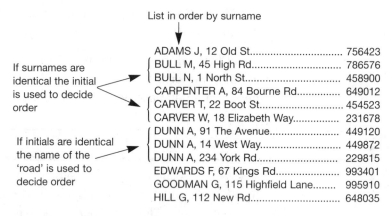

List in order by surname

ADAMS J, 12 Old St.............................. 756423
BULL M, 45 High Rd.............................. 786576
BULL N, 1 North St................................ 458900
CARPENTER A, 84 Bourne Rd.............. 649012
CARVER T, 22 Boot St............................ 454523
CARVER W, 18 Elizabeth Way................ 231678
DUNN A, 91 The Avenue........................ 449120
DUNN A, 14 West Way........................... 449872
DUNN A, 234 York Rd............................ 229815
EDWARDS F, 67 Kings Rd..................... 993401
GOODMAN G, 115 Highfield Lane........ 995910
HILL G, 112 New Rd.............................. 648035

If surnames are identical the initial is used to decide order

If initials are identical the name of the 'road' is used to decide order

Figure 2.1 **Alphabetical ordering**

ACTIVITY 2.3

Suggest three different organisations that would keep information on a database. What type of information would they keep?

Spreadsheets

The term 'spreadsheet' describes a very large sheet of paper traditionally used by accountants to record financial transactions. Nowadays, this is done using an IT system.

A spreadsheet has **rows** and **columns** (Figure 2.2). Rows are usually numbered: 1, 2, 3, etc. and the columns are usually lettered: A, B, C, etc. Where rows and columns intersect we have a **cell** (sometimes called a slot).

ACTIVITY 2.4

Think of three different organisations which might use a spreadsheet package. What calculations would these organisations do using their spreadsheet?

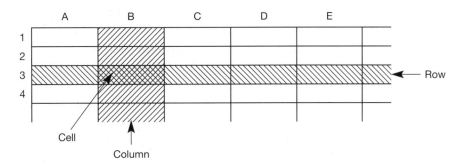

Figure 2.2 **Parts of a spreadsheet**

Graphics

Graphics packages are used to process images.

Painting and **drawing** packages allow you to create your own images, edit them and produce a finished printout. These may be used to create illustrations for a book, or to design advertising material.

Graphic packages also allow 'retouching' of photographs – adding, removing or recolouring parts of the image.

In **computer-aided design** (CAD), drawings are created to scale, using the computer to calculate sizes and to present different views of a design.

ACTIVITY 2.5

Think of three different organisations which would use graphics packages. Which type of package would these organisations use, and what would they produce using the software?

Tasks

There are four tasks that most organisations are faced with, and for which they may use IT systems:

1. document processing
2. data handling
3. calculations
4. graphic design

You need to know which applications packages they use to do these tasks.

Integrated packages offer some or all of the five common applications within the one software package. However, it is important for you to know the main purpose of each individual applications package. You will then be able to choose the best applications package for any given task. Even though you could use some spreadsheet packages to store a database, it is important to know that the main purpose of a spreadsheet package is to process numerical data, and that the main purpose of a database package is to process structured data. Using a spreadsheet package to process a database is a poor choice.

There are also some specialist applications, like payroll, which would not be tackled using any of the five common applications.

Document processing

Documents are usually processed using a word processing package. If the document includes images, a DTP package may be needed.

Chapter 4 looks in detail at processing documents, especially how you can produce them. Here we concentrate on what kind of document you might want to produce.

For most organisations, documents can be divided into two main types: internal and external.

Internal documents

Internal documents are ones which stay within an organisation and are not seen by people outside the organisation. One example is the memorandum – or memo for short.

ACTIVITY 2.6

Look back at your notes from Activity 2.1. Which of the four documents you listed are internal documents? Think of four other internal documents that might be produced on a word processing package. If possible, collect some examples of internal documents.

External documents

Most external documents are produced on word processors. External documents are ones which are sent from or received by an organisation. The presentation of these documents is more important, because people outside an organisation can use them to judge an organisation. Companies care about the image they create and much time and money is often spent on designing a company logo that presents the image the company wants.

ACTIVITY 2.7

Look back at your notes from Activity 2.1. Which of the four documents you listed are external documents? Make a list of eight different types of documents which would be produced on a word processor, and then sent to someone outside an organisation. If possible, collect an example of each type of document.

Data handling

Data handling is the processing of records in a database. We call this **structured data** and consider the practical problems of processing this data in greater detail in Chapter 7.

All organisations collect data – about their employees, customers and suppliers. Some organisations also collect information about their competitors.

Some organisations have reason to collect data because of the nature of their business. For example, an estate agent would keep details about the houses they have to sell, as well as the people who have registered with them as looking for a new home.

ACTIVITY 2.8

Look back at your notes from Activity 2.3. For each of your three organisations make a list of five different types of data they might keep and suggest reasons for keeping this data on a database.

Calculations

Processing numerical information is usually done on a spreadsheet. We look at the practical problems of this in greater detail in Chapter 6.

Some organisations use a spreadsheet package for planning and costing purposes.

ACTIVITY 2.9

Look back at your notes from Activity 2.4. For each of your three organisations, make a list of three different uses of a spreadsheet package.

Graphic design

The practical aspects of graphic design are covered in Chapter 5. Here we look at why you might use a graphics package, and what you would use it for.

ACTIVITY 2.10

One of the most common uses of graphic software is in storing a company logo. What is a company logo? Collect ten sample logos.

Graphic design is supported by many different types of graphics software. Once you have finalised your ideas you have several choices:

- You can use a **drawing** or **painting package** to draw your own artwork.
- You can use **clip-art** – ready-drawn artwork – to paste into your document.
- You can **scan** in images using some software.

How you store your images may affect what you can do with them later. There are two main types of graphic image: bit-map (or raster) and vector.

Bit-map graphics

Some images are stored as **bit-map** images. Generally painting packages produce bit-map images. Scanned images are also stored in bit-map format.

In the simplest systems, an image is stored as a series of bits, each one storing the value 0 or 1 to mean white or black. The image is divided into rows and columns of **pixels**. The pixel is the smallest unit of an image; it will be either black or white. Figure 2.3 gives a simple example.

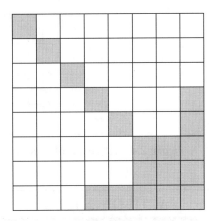

Pattern is: 1000 0000 0100 0000
                  0010 0000 0001 0001
                  0000 1001 0000 0111
                  0000 0111 0001 1111

Figure 2.3 **A image coded using 0s and 1s**

On more complex systems, shades of grey or colour are recognised. For these systems, more storage space is needed to remember all the pixels that make up the image. To make it possible to store very complex image information, image compression techniques have been invented. These are very complicated – and very clever – ways of storing the image data.

ACTIVITY 2.11

Decode these patterns to see what images are stored. Figure 2.4 (overleaf) gives the correct images.

Pattern 1: 0011 1110 0100 0001   Pattern 2: 0000 0100 0000 1100
                  1000 0001 0000 0001   0001 0100 0010 0100
                  0001 1110 0001 0000   0100 0100 1111 1111
                  0000 0000 0001 0000   0000 0100 0000 0100

Apart from storage problems, bit-map images have another drawback. Because the image is made from black and white or coloured pixels any increase in scale will result in a poorer quality image. The dots in the picture are of a fixed size, and so when made larger the overall effect can be lost. For instance, straight lines can seem to become jagged. This is called loss of **resolution**.

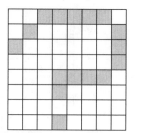 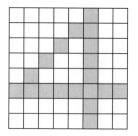

Figure 2.4 **Activity 2.11 – decoded patterns**

ACTIVITY 2.12

Think of three examples of complex images that are stored on an IT system.

Vector graphics

Vector graphics are stored in a completely different way. Instead of recording each pixel of an image, the image is created from **graphic elements** and details of these are stored instead.

An image produced using a drawing package will be stored as a vector graphic. The drawing will be made from graphic elements such as **lines**, **circles** and **rectangles**. The IT system stores the minimum information needed to reproduce the graphic elements. For example, the data for a circle would include the position of its centre and its radius. Other information might include the type of line used to draw the circle, and whether it was filled with a colour.

The benefit of vector graphics is that you can scale the image up (or down) without any loss of resolution. It also requires a lot less storage space.

ACTIVITY 2.13

Look back at your notes from Activity 2.5. For each of your three organisations, write more details on why you think they choose to use a graphics package. What alternatives do they have?

Benefits of using common applications

As with all computerised systems, the user expects benefits such as:

- speed
- efficiency

- cost
- accuracy
- quality

Usually, it is a combination of these benefits which persuades an organisation to use an application package rather than tackle a task by hand. However, here we consider them one by one.

Speed

IT systems process data much faster than humans:

- A standard letter can be produced and personally addressed to all customers in a fraction of the time it would take to type them out.
- An advertisement could be created using a DTP package, and different designs tried out, much quicker than drawing everything by hand.
- A database package could be used to identify all patients who had been prescribed a particular drug much quicker than if someone had to hunt through all the medical records.
- In a spreadsheet, the formulae can be recalculated in a fraction of a second. A human would take much longer.
- A graphics package could be used to scan in a manager's signature rather than the manager trying to 'draw' the signature using a drawing package. This signature could then be incorporated into all letters and save the manager having to sign them all by hand.

ACTIVITY 2.14

Look back through your notes written for previous activities. Which of your organisations use IT to save time? Which package do they use and for what purpose? Can you think of some more examples?

Efficiency

IT systems offer greater efficiency than humans. This is mostly because programs are written which specify that certain things are done in a certain order. Nothing is missed out or overlooked. It is quite possible for a human to be efficient, but not all the time! We can become tired towards the end of a long day, be side-tracked by other things going on around us, or just make slips. Once the IT system has been programmed, there are none of these problems.

when all the benefits are considered, most organisations would decide IT was a worthwhile investment.

A business user may decide to purchase an IT system for many reasons:

- To keep up with competitors.
- To cope with an increasing workload without taking on more staff.
- To process work more quickly and thus increase productivity of existing staff.
- To improve efficiency and therefore to ensure greater levels of success.
- To gain access to information available, e.g. on the internet.
- To improve quality of material produced by the organisation and thus to improve the organisation's image.
- To tackle problems that could not be done manually.

ACTIVITY 2.16

The first use of a computer to take a census resulted in the data being available before it was time to take the next census. Try to find out more about this early use of IT.

ACTIVITY 2.17

The use of credit cards to pay for goods is a more recent example of a problem that could be solved only through using IT. If the system had been a manual one, the credit card companies could not have coped with the volume of transactions. Can you think of any other examples where IT has made something possible?

The reasons for using an IT solution can be difficult to measure in terms of cost. It could be quite easy to calculate the savings possible if ten clerks are to be replaced by one data entry clerk and a PC. But how much is it worth to have a competitive edge? How much is it worth to have up-to-date information at your fingertips? In cases like this, the decision-makers often find they have no choice but to use the IT solution, almost regardless of cost.

ACTIVITY 2.18

Look back through your notes written for previous activities. Which of your organisations use IT to cut costs? Which package do they use and for what purpose? Can you think of some more examples?

ACTIVITY 2.19

Can you think of any examples where organisations have invested heavily in IT even though they had no guarantee of success?

Accuracy

Compared with humans, calculations made by an IT system are accurate. However, because it is still humans that input the data, write and test the software and so on, the output is not necessarily correct.

Garbage in, garbage out

To try to prevent data being input incorrectly, two techniques can be used: validation and verification.

Validation

Validation checks the data. Is it reasonable? It is within range? Has it the expected type of characters – letters for surnames, digits for telephone numbers?

- If you complete an application and put your date of birth as 66/1/1970, when this is keyed a validation check should see that this is not a valid date. January has only 31 days.
- If you complete an application and put your date of birth as 6/1/1996, when this is keyed a validation check should see that this is a valid date, but that it cannot be a valid date of birth. The validation routine in the software should be written to look for this type of error.

Validation *cannot* check the accuracy of what has been keyed. However, because the validation checks can be computerised, it is an easy check to make to identify data which must be incorrect.

Verification

Verification involves comparing what has been input with the original data. This does try to check the accuracy – of the keyboarding. It still cannot check if the data is truly accurate.

For instance, if you complete an application and put your date of birth as 6/1/1975, when this is keyed a validation check will not reject it. It is a valid date and it could be a valid date of birth. When the keyboard operator compares what is on the screen with your form, they will know they have keyed it correctly. However, you may have been confused when filling in the form and, actually, your date of birth is June 1st 1975.

Maintaining the integrity of data

After data has been input – hopefully accurately – care still needs to be taken to make sure it does not become corrupted at a later date. This is called maintaining the **integrity** of the data. Corruption can happen in many ways:

- The computer (or a network) can crash, due to power problems or some other electrical connection problem. This may cause loss of data in memory. If the organisation has taken the precaution of performing back-ups, this should not be too much of a problem.
- Errors can happen with the medium, e.g. the disk may develop a fault. Again, back-ups should allow an organisation to recover from this type of disaster.
- There may be errors (called **bugs**) in the software which cause data to be overwritten. This is a disaster, because usually it can go undetected for some time, and back-ups will then not be helpful because they too will be corrupted. Prevention, rather than cure, is

the way to avoid this problem, by thoroughly testing all software before use. Even if it is purchased from the largest manufacturer of software in the world, it can still have bugs.

- Data may be corrupted intentionally by someone with access to the IT system (authorised or not). Where access is authorised, an organisation will have problems identifying who is causing data corruption, unless they have issued **user ID codes** and kept an **audit trail** of all users on the system.

- **Viruses** may also be introduced, and these can cause severe disruption to an organisation. This might be avoided if employees are not allowed to use their own disks on IT systems at work, and if virus checks are made on all disks introduced to the system.

- **Unauthorised access** should be avoidable. Most IT systems have **password** control. Networked systems include **access controls** preventing access to certain areas. **Hackers** are prevented from understanding the data being transmitted, even if they do gain access to the signal, because the data is **encrypted**.

- There may be a natural disaster – fire, flood, earthquake – but this tends to cause loss of data rather than simple corruption of some data. Keeping copies of files in fireproof safes may be helpful. Sprinkler systems may prevent a fire spreading. The worst disasters, however, are difficult to plan for.

ACTIVITY 2.20

You may have seen the film where a computer programmer 'fixes' the payroll program so that all the money rounded down to the nearest cent (it was in America) from everyone else's pay was added to his. Can you remember any real life incident of computer fraud reported in the newspapers?

Accuracy using a word processing package

Word processing packages usually have a spellchecker facility which can help the user to present a more accurate document. The spellchecker only checks individual words, not the content of the document. If the facts are incorrect but correctly spelt, the spellchecker will not notice!

Also if you miskey a word, and as a result enter another word that is correctly spelt, the spell checker will not notice. This poem gives lots of examples of errors which will not be spotted by a spellchecker:

Eye have a spelling chequer
It came with my Pea Sea
It plainly marques for my revue
Mistakes eye cannot sea.
I've run this poem threw it,
Eye am sure your plea's too no,
It's letter perfect in it's weigh,
My chequer tolled me sew!

(Reproduced courtesy of the Midland Bank Pensioners' Association)

Accuracy using a DTP package

If a DTP package is used to integrate text (produced on a word processing package) and graphics (produced on a graphics package) the accuracy checks on those packages should already have been used.

In addition, the facility to use style sheets will allow organisations to have a standard layout for their publications. Standardisation reduces the margin for error by the operator.

Accuracy using a database package

Using a database entails a lot of data entry. For this, the password controls mentioned earlier and the validation and verification of data during entry are essential.

The design of a database helps to ensure the accuracy of data; at least it should encourage **consistency of data**.

- **Coding** of data is used wherever possible. The operator does not key fresh data, but chooses from a list of options. This reduces the chance of the operator miskeying.
- Relational databases allow data that would normally be repeated to be stored only once. Databases **minimise data duplication**. All reports produced using this data item would retrieve it from a single location. This does mean that if it is wrong it appears wrong everywhere, but if it is correct, it is correct everywhere.
- Using coding and/or relational databases means that if some data has to change it is only changed in one location. The chance of changing data incorrectly is still present, but lower than if it had to be changed in many different locations.

For example, if a database holds details of a college timetable, a coding system will be used for all the subjects on the curriculum. The operator will be presented with a list of options: IT, Leisure and Tourism, Science and so on.

Also, because IT systems process data more quickly, greater throughput of work can be achieved by a worker and this increases his or her productivity.

- A document prepared a year ago can become the basis for an updated version. Although the detail may change, the layout would be much the same. It makes more sense to use the document and amend it than to start from scratch.
- A DTP package allows the user to recalculate page positioning automatically, pull in artwork from many different files, and use lots of different colours. Instead of a cluttered desk, the designer has a PC.
- A database provides the opportunity to store information in such a way that you can ask any question and get a quick reply. The important thing is for the database designer to know in advance what type of question you will be wanting to ask. Then the database can be set up in a way that will allow this to happen. The design of the database is very important. It determines how efficient the user of the database can be.
- A spreadsheet allows a user to make 'What if?' enquiries. This means the user sets out all the things that affect a situation: the costs, time-scales and so on. Then the user can change one thing and see what effect this has on everything else. Will the deadline be achievable? Will the project be completed within budget? This software offers the planner the information needed to make sound decisions and ensure that future efforts are not wasted.
- A graphic design package can draw circles, of any given size, more accurately than a human. It is rare that this degree of accuracy matters so much that an organisation will decide to buy software, but it does mean the quality of presentation can be as high as possible.

ACTIVITY 2.15

Look back through your notes written for previous activities. Which of your organisations use IT to improve efficiency? Which package do they use and for what purpose? Can you think of some more examples?

Cost

The initial cost of an IT system including all the necessary peripherals and software may seem exorbitant – especially to parents! However,

The operator needs only to key the first letter (which is quicker as well as more accurate).

In the student's record, a code for the subject is stored, rather than the full name of the subject (this also saves data storage space). Whenever the subject title has to be printed out, e.g. for individual timetables, for teachers' reports and so on, the original keyed version of the subject, in full, can appear.

If it is decided that IT should appear in full as 'Information Technology' then a single change, in the coding table, is all that is needed.

Accuracy using a spreadsheet package

Data entered into a single cell on a spreadsheet can be one of three types:

- Text – if the first character you key is a letter, the spreadsheet software will assume it is text; no checks can be made on this data.
- Numeric – if the first character is a digit (or '–', '+' or some other arithmetic symbol) the spreadsheet software will assume the data you are entering is a number, and will check that it obeys the normal rules for a number.
- If you key a special symbol to indicate the start of a formula (e.g. '@' or '+') the spreadsheet software will accept all you key until the final 'return'. It then checks if the formula matches the syntax of acceptable commands. If not it will reject it, and probably beep at you.

When the data is displayed further checks are made, to make sure the reader is not misinformed. If the width of the column is too narrow to display the data in full, text will be truncated (the end cut off) but numeric data, and the results of any formula will be replaced by a series of '*' (or some other error symbol) to show that there is a problem. If only the start (or end) of a number was shown, it could be confusing. Instead the user is warned that the column is not wide enough, and the data will only appear in full if steps are taken to alter the width of these columns.

Accuracy using a graphics package

Graphics software has tools which allow a user with little drawing skill to create accurate shapes. Editing tools allow amendment by scaling, rotating and so on. If you make a mistake, you have an eraser to rub it out.

One feature of all software application packages is that you can save your work, and reload it at a later time. This can be useful if you are trying out different designs. You can save a design using one filename, carry on working on it and save the later version with a different filename. If at any stage the newer design 'goes wrong' you can save yourself work correcting it by just reloading an earlier version.

ACTIVITY 2.21

Look back through all your notes written for previous activities. Which of your organisations use IT to improve accuracy? Which package do they use and for what purpose? Can you think of some more examples?

Quality

It is important that information is accurate, up-to-date, relevant and timely. All these are possible using IT systems, and they are all factors which contribute to the quality of the material being produced.

However, the term 'quality' is also applied to the finished product: the letter, advertisement or printed report.

- The quality of a letter most often depends on the communications skills of the writer rather than the word processing package itself. Has the message been well expressed? A word processing package allows you to draft and redraft a letter until what is said exactly matches what you want to say. Most word processing packages offer a thesaurus facility which suggests similar words so that you can find just the right word to use.
- The quality of a spreadsheet is dependent on the accuracy of the formulae, and the data entered. The spreadsheet package cannot offer more than the accuracy checks mentioned earlier.
- The quality of the reports produced from a database depend on the design of the database, the accuracy of the data entered and the skill of the person interrogating the database. The software itself does not add to the quality.
- The **presentation quality** available on a DTP system outshines anything that might be produced manually by most of us. This is the one application where IT has transformed how an organisation presents itself to others.

ACTIVITY 2.22

Look back through your notes written for previous activities. Which of your organisations use IT to improve quality? Which packages do they use and for what purpose? Can you think of some more examples?

Limitations of using common applications

It would be wonderful if the use of IT brought only good things. But, unfortunately, there are also limitations to consider! These may include:

- initial development time
- costs
- security
- speed of processing small quantities of data

Initial development time

Initial development is the time required before any IT system can be implemented. Having decided to use IT to solve a problem, it can take a long time to acquire the hardware and software, train staff, test the system and transfer the manual system onto the computerised IT system. The transfer period can be a very stressful time, with staff trying to continue with the normal day-to-day work as well as starting the new system.

ACTIVITY 2.23

Try to find out how long an organisation took to develop a system.

Costs

We looked at costs earlier in this chapter – then the user was trying to minimise costs by using IT.

Here we need to look at all the costs which arise when you decide to use IT. The main costs are for purchases:

- the hardware (computer equipment, workstations and suitable chairs)

- the software (the application packages and operating system, and probably a user interface)

Other costs include:

- retraining present staff to use the IT system
- employing staff with the necessary skills to install and run the IT system

Security

Using an IT system to store data increases, rather than decreases, security problems:

- Information kept on paper is bulky; information kept on floppy disk is more portable.
- Information stored on paper is located within a building which may be protected by burglar alarms, security patrols, locks and grilles. Information on a computer network may be accessed by a hacker situated a great distance from the building and the files themselves.
- Information stolen from paper files tends to leave a trace. There will have been a break-in. If information is stolen from computer files it is very difficult to trace who did it, or even to know that it has happened.
- To remove a file of paper and copy it would take some time. To take a copy of a computer file takes hardly any time at all.

We have already mentioned the need for security, to maintain the integrity of data. There is another reason for protecting data: the Data Protection Act (1984) sets out obligations of users of data, which include taking adequate precautions to protect the data.

The methods used to protect data fall into two types: physical and logical methods.

Physical access control

These include:

- building security – perimeter fence, entry barrier controlled by a security guard
- computer area security – locked doors with keys allocated only to a select few personnel, passcards to allow entry to sensitive areas
- computer terminal security – keyboard locks

If someone gains physical access, the next barrier will be the logical access control.

Logical access control

Logical access methods refer to those controlled by software:

- **User ID codes** are used to log onto a system. These codes are unique to an individual, so each time access to files is made this can be recorded on the **audit trail**.
- **Password systems** are a second barrier. These are chosen by the user, and should be kept secret. Password control protects the user. Even if someone else knows your ID code, they will also need to know your password to gain entry to the system.
- **User access level control** uses the user ID code to allow access only to certain areas of information and to certain functions. This may be divided into low priority (can view data but not change it), medium priority (can change day-to-day data, but cannot access more sensitive information) and high priority (total access to all data).
- Individual files can also be protected in a similar way.

Security methods

Apart from setting up the various physical and logical access controls, organisations will try to set up systems which will help them to know when there has been a security breach, and to recover from any data loss. These include:

- **Back-up procedures** – taking copies of data and holding them in a secure place.
- Keeping an **audit trail** – recording details of each time that data is accessed, noting the user ID code, time of access, and details of changes made.

It is also important for staff to realise how they can improve security:

- Following security procedures to gain entry to the computer area, and not lending their key to anyone else.
- Following security procedures to gain access to computer files, and not telling anyone else the password currently in use.
- Keeping confidential any information seen while working on an IT system.
- Not using personal disks on the work system (in case viruses are introduced).

Speed of processing small quantities of data

Using IT to solve a data processing problem is usually the best option.

However, there are situations when IT is not the most effective or cost-efficient option.

IT solutions rely on processing high volumes of data quicker than a human can. If the problem involves only a few records, it would be quicker to do it manually, and cheaper to use a person for 15 minutes per week than to install a PC and buy all the software to go with it. Calculating the payroll for a workforce of three would not warrant using an IT solution.

IT solutions rely on doing the same thing over and over again. If the problem involves many different situations, and requires a high level of skill for each different task, it may not be possible to program a computer to do the same task. Speaking to customers who telephone with enquiries is a good example. Some theatre box office lines have a prerecorded message; the caller can use the touch telephone to choose an option to hear about certain films on show. This service meets the needs of most callers, but at some time a real human is needed to communicate with the caller. Expert systems try to copy how an expert would solve a problem. These are being developed for use in doctor's surgeries, to help diagnose what is wrong with a patient and to prescribe a course of action. These systems are very complex and, as yet, untried.

The main reason for *not* using one of the five common applications studied in this chapter is the volume of data being too low to warrant computerisation.

ACTIVITY 2.24

List the four main limitations of using IT solutions, giving examples for each one.

The evidence indicators

To prove you have covered the material of this element you need to produce a list:

- identifying common applications of IT, with at least one example of each
- describing the benefits and limitations of using the common applications

A summary is also needed comparing the suitability of the application for different tasks.

The notes made in answer to the many activities in this chapter should include enough evidence for your portfolio. Read through your notes again, and present them in a summarised form. Produce this list on a word processing package; this document can then serve as a reminder for revision prior to your external test and as evidence for Element 2.1: Process documents.

3 Demonstrate the use of an information technology system

Introduction

This chapter covers the material needed for Element 1.3: Demonstrate the use of an information technology system.

An IT system includes the following:

- hardware
- software
- infrastructure
- staff
- accommodation

The performance criteria state that the student must:

1. Identify the **components** of an information technology system.
2. Describe the **purpose of the components** of an information technology system.
3. Identify the reasons for using information technology to carry out a task.
4. **Find** required stored data and **use** an information technology system.
5. Present output in a way which meets **requirements**.

The knowledge range

To meet the performance criteria, you *must* cover the range. The words shown in bold in the performance criteria above highlight the skills and knowledge you will need and so we will now consider each of these in turn.

Components

An IT system includes hardware and software. The software falls into two main types:

- operating systems software
- applications software

There are five main hardware components of an IT system:

- input devices
- output devices
- main processing unit
- memory devices
- storage devices

These are shown in Figure 3.1.

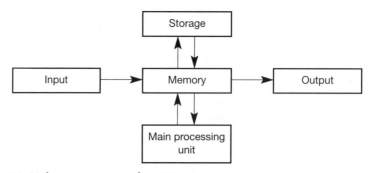

Figure 3.1 **Main components of an IT system**

ACTIVITY 3.1

Make a copy of Figure 3.1 and label it with the items of equipment in your own IT system.

Input devices

Input devices allow data to be entered for the first time into an IT system. They are also called **primary input devices**, and include:

- keyboard (QWERTY keyboards, keypads, concept keyboards)
- mouse/trackerball
- sensor

It does *not* include:

- disk – these devices store data and are used for **secondary input**
- touch sensitive screen – these are called I/O devices, i.e. they are both input and output devices.

Keyboard

A keyboard (Figure 3.2) is the most common input device for use with general purpose computers. They have a number of keys, but not necessarily the same number for all computers; nor is the arrangement of keys always the same. Most keyboards have three parts:

- The main part of the keyboard is likely to be arranged as on a traditional typewriter, i.e. a **QWERTY keyboard**.
- Another section may be arranged as a block of keys including the digits 0–9, plus the arithmetic symbols for add, subtract, multiply and divide, and an enter key. This part of the keyboard is called a **numeric keypad**.
- There may also be special keys including, at least, enter (or return), escape (ESC), control (CTRL) and some function keys. What these keys do depends on the software being used rather than the hardware.

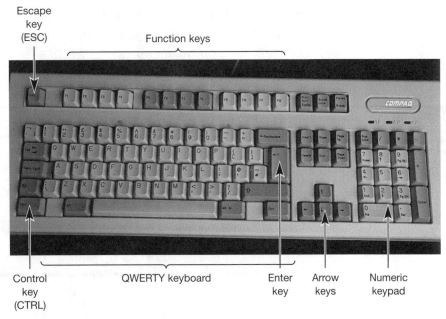

Figure 3.2 **Standard keyboard layout**

A **keystrip** is a piece of plastic or card used with a keyboard. It labels the operations performed by function keys within specific programs. For example, in a word processor the function key F4 might have the function Search/Replace.

ACTIVITY 3.2

Using two different software packages, note what effect pressing the function key F4 has in each one. (You may find that the effect depends on where you are within the package.)

Keypads
Keypads are handheld input devices often used in supermarkets to check on the price of an item. They have smaller sets of keys and a small display area.

Concept keyboards
Concept keyboards were originally introduced for children (or adults) who had problems with the small keys on a QWERTY keyboard. The keys were much larger which made it easier to press the correct key. Later, the design was extended to allow a push-button choice of many options. Nowadays, they are seen on most shop tills, especially in restaurants and bars. When a key is pressed, it relates to a choice, e.g. 'large fries' or 'chocolate milkshake', and the price of the item is automatically displayed. This type of input allows the manager to preset the prices and saves the assistant from remembering the costs of every item on the menu.

ACTIVITY 3.3

If you already have experience of using a concept keyboard, write notes on how to program it and how to operate it. Next time you visit a local newsagent, a greengrocers or a fast-food restaurant, check whether they use a concept keyboard. When you have found a concept keyboard in use, ask the manager how complicated it is to program in the prices. Ask the shop assistant how easy it is to use.

Mouse

A mouse is another computer input device (Figure 3.3), usually connected to the computer by a thin cable. Moving the mouse across a flat surface (or mouse mat) causes a cursor, or pointer, on the display screen to move.

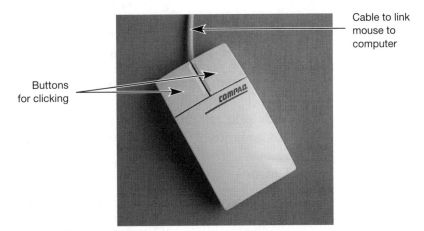

Cable to link
mouse to
computer

Buttons
for clicking

COMPAQ

Figure 3.3 **Typical mouse**

A **trackerball** is a similar input device and is used to do the same things as a mouse. It is a ball, set into a cup, which can be made to roll in any direction by using a finger or the palm of a hand, depending on the size of the ball. The movements of the ball are mirrored on the screen by a pointer and finger-operated switches work in the same way as mouse buttons. Trackerballs are now sometimes mounted on laptop computers, being easier to use here than a mouse.

A mouse has one, or more, finger-operated switches, called (mouse) **buttons**.

- Pressing a mouse button is called **clicking**, because this usually produces a 'click' sound. If the user clicks when the pointer controlled by the mouse is on an icon, or a screen button, then the operation represented by that icon (or button) is **selected**.
- Some software expects the mouse button to be pressed twice in quick succession, this is **double clicking**. A single click may have one effect while double clicking may have another. (What effect these have will depend upon where the pointer is on the screen and what software is being used.)

Dragging – moving the mouse while holding down a button – is used to move an area of a screen display, which may be text or some part of a graphic display, from one location to another. Before such movement can take place, the area concerned has to be defined, e.g. by highlighting text, or by marking the boundaries of a graphic item. Moving things around in this way is sometimes referred to as **drag-and-drop editing**. This may also be used to copy, as well as move, part of a screen display. One example of dragging is moving the icon for a file from one sub-directory to another as a way of repositioning the file within the computer's file system. Another would be moving a graphic item from an application running in one window on the screen to a different application running in another window.

Mouse operations, such as clicking, dragging or combining these with the use of keys on the keyboard, provide a wide range of possible options at any moment. Actions, such as pressing or releasing the mouse buttons, are sometimes called **mouse events**.

Sensor

Sensors are used all around us, usually without people realising.

- When you use a lift, many sensors control the opening and closing of the doors and the movement between floors.
- When you use a car wash, sensors detect the position of the car.
- When you leave a supermarket, the doors open automatically for you.
- At night, lights turn on when someone approaches a security sensor.
- Alarms sound when smoke is sensed in a building.

ACTIVITY 3.4

Make a list of ten situations where sensors are used to trigger some reaction.

A sensor is a device which outputs electrical signals when changes occur in its environment. For example, a sensor could notice a change in heat, light, pH (acidity), sound or movement. It therefore **senses** a change in the environment.

A **transducer** is an electronic component which converts one form of energy to another. For example:

- A **thermistor** converts a temperature into electrical energy with a varying voltage.
- A **photo-cell** converts brightness of illuminations into a voltage.

The term transducer is generally used to describe devices which produce electricity rather than those which convert electricity into another form of energy.

A sensor is therefore a transducer which responds to a physical property such as pressure, rate of flow of a liquid, or humidity.

The sensor produces an electrical output which is either **analogue** or **digital**.

Some sensors, called **passive devices**, require no external electrical source. Those which require an external voltage are called **active devices**.

ACTIVITY 3.5

Using your list of ten sensors, decide what type each one is. Does it sense heat, light, pressure or something else? Can you tell? If not, do some checking and try to find out what is happening.

Output devices

Output devices allow data to be displayed or printed. These include:

- VDU
- printer
- controlling device

VDU

VDU stands for **visual display unit**. Sometimes, it is more simply called a **screen** or **monitor** (Figure 3.4).

The screen displays information using a cathode ray tube. This is similar to a TV except it does not receive TV signals. Instead signals are sent from the computer for display on the screen.

Monitors can be **monochrome**, displaying one colour, such as white, green or orange on a dark (usually black) background. **Colour monitors** display in many different colours according to the type of screen and computer being used.

The **prompt** is a character (or sometimes a message) displayed on a screen to indicate that the operator is expected to do something, e.g. to input data into the system. Sometimes this visual prompt is emphasised by a sound, such as a beep.

The **resolution** (or apparent clearness or quality) of the screen depends on the number of **pixels** displayed on the screen. On TV screens, the resolution is approximately 320 by 200 pixels. This means the screen is split into a grid of 320 units by 200 units, each cell of the grid having one colour (or shade of grey in a black and white screen). This is fine for displaying teletext. On a computer screen, better resolution is needed. For a low resolution screen, say one measuring 36 centimetres across the diagonal, the number of pixels may be 640 by 400. For a high

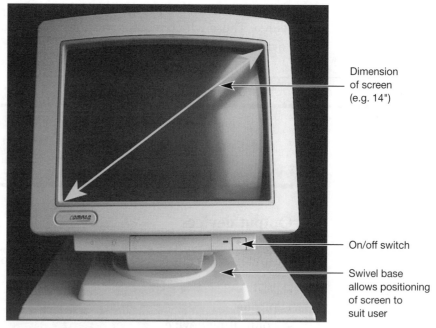

Dimension
of screen
(e.g. 14")

On/off switch

Swivel base
allows positioning
of screen to
suit user

Figure 3.4 **Typical monitor or display**

resolution screen – needed for professional graphics – you would need
1024 by 768 pixels. The higher the resolution, the better the quality of
the picture, and the higher the cost of the screen and the amount of
computer memory the display needs.

Laptop computers (Figure 3.5) have built-in screens, which are
usually quite small and flat. Some screens are made from two thin
sheets of glass with liquid crystals between them; these are called
liquid crystal displays. The resolution is not good, but may suit the
user of a portable computer.

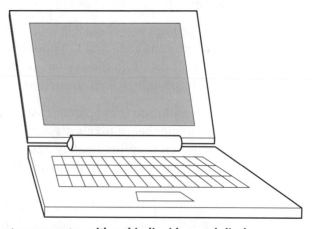

Figure 3.5 **Laptop computer with a thin liquid crystal display**

Printer

Printers are used to produce **hardcopy** of data as a permanent record. There are two main types of printer in use nowadays: character printers and page printers.

Character printers print one character at a time. Examples of character printers are dot matrix printers, daisy wheel printers and ink jet printers. Dot matrix printers and daisy wheel printers are both **impact printers**; they involve a printhead hitting the paper through an inked tape. Impact printers are noisy and slow.

Dot matrix printers (Figure 3.6) form each character from a grid of pins. The more pins that are used, the greater the resolution and therefore the quality of printing. Most dot matrix printers also offer two modes: draft and 'near letter quality' (NLQ). NLQ printing involves printing the same character twice, close to each other; this gives a better printed effect, but takes twice as long.

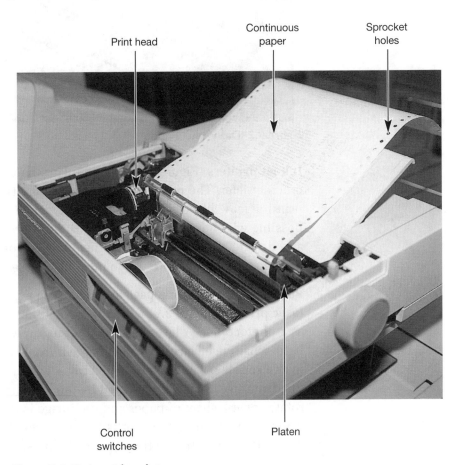

Figure 3.6 **Dot matrix printer**

Daisy wheel printers (Figure 3.7) have their print characters on a wheel which spins before printing each character. This makes it very slow. However, the quality is very good, and different fonts are available (although you do have to change the daisy wheel each time).

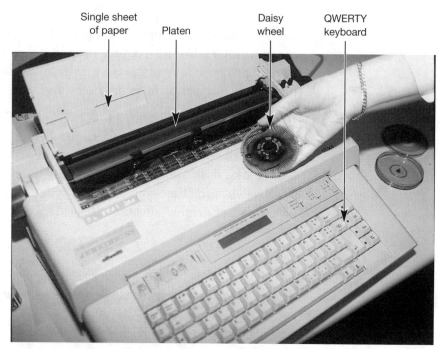

Single sheet of paper   Platen   Daisy wheel   QWERTY keyboard

Figure 3.7 **Daisy wheel printer**

Ink jet printers (Figure 3.8) 'squirt' ink at the page and so they are much quieter. The paper must be a good quality otherwise the printing may 'bleed' and the end result can be poor. Colour printing is possible which offers good opportunities to produce excellent artwork and designs. Ink jet printers are inexpensive but they are still slow, so a page printer is of more use to most businesses.

Page printers print one page at a time. The most common form is the **laser printer** (Figure 3.9) which works on the same kind of principles as a photocopier. A laser beam is used to 'draw' the shape onto a light-sensitive electrostatically charged drum. This drum then rotates over a source of toner – powdered ink – which sticks to the parts of the drum that have been affected by the laser beam. Finally, the drum rotates over a sheet of paper and the image is transferred from the drum to the paper. The paper is heated as the drum rotates and this makes the toner stick to the paper as it passes.

Most laser printers offer good resolution – about 300 dpi (dots per inch) – but they are expensive to buy and to run. Toner cartridges

Paper tray   Instructions   Controls

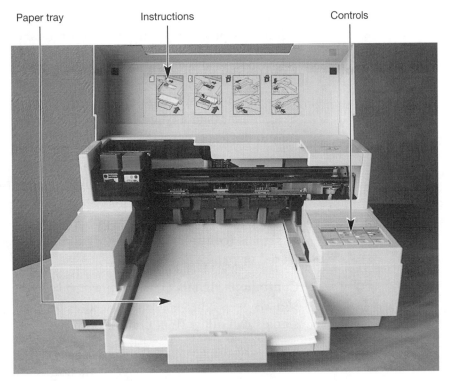

Figure 3.8 **Ink jet printer**

Paper trays allow
choice of size of paper   Controls

Figure 3.9 **Laser printer**

need replacing frequently, and the running costs are higher than for dot matrix printers or daisy wheel printers.

Controlling device

If the output from a computer is to go to another machine rather than to a human, then a controlling device is used instead of the usual output device.

At the back of a computer, there are a number of **ports** (Figure 3.10) These allow cables to be connected to other items of equipment. The **output ports** allow signals to be sent from the computer; these are called **control signals**. Different kinds of ports allow different kinds of signals (continuous or pulsed) along different types of cable (serial or parallel).

Continuous signals are sent in a steady voltage stream; **pulsed signals** are sent as a series of signals broken by gaps in time. Pulsed signals can allow finer control of movement, e.g. of a robot arm.

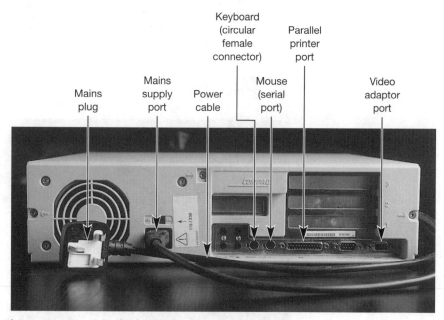

Figure 3.10 **Ports in the back of a typical PC**

Serial cables can only take one bit of information at a time; **parallel** cable looks like a ribbon, and can take several bits of information at the same time. Parallel connections will allow faster transfer of information.

There are two main types of controlling device: relays and actuators.

A **relay** is a switch which can be turned on or off by an electrical signal from the computer. This relay can then be used to control lights or motors, turning them on or off.

An **actuator** is any device which results in a movement when it receives an electrical signal. It therefore transfers the electrical signal into a movement and makes something happen.

Main processor unit

The main processor unit is the central part of every IT system. All other items are referred to as **peripherals** – things on the side.

The main processor – also called the **central processing unit** (CPU) – controls every piece of hardware attached to it, and all software running in it (Figure 3.11).

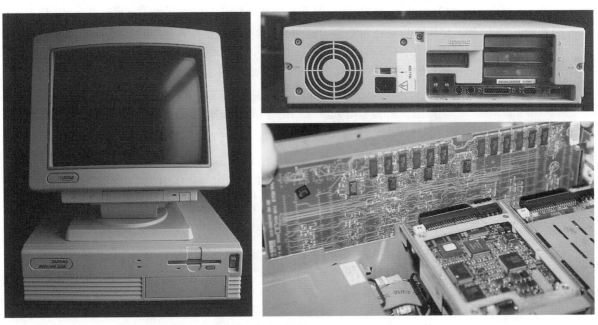

Figure 3.11 **Front, rear and inside views of a typical PC**

The ability of the CPU is measured in terms of its speed of processing; the faster the processor, the more powerful the IT system. The amount of memory (RAM and ROM – see page 79) is also important. Generally speaking, the more powerful machines are more expensive, though as time passes, newer machines are far more powerful than their predecessors and yet the prices do not rise at the same rate.

Software

The software – the elements of the system that are not hardware – is what makes the IT system do what you, the user, want it to do. All makes of computers are different, and the manufacturers design them to have different features. This is a good selling point for the manufacturer, but means that each type of computer has different software needs.

There are two main types of software: operating systems and applications software.

Operating system

Operating systems 'operate the system'. Without an operating system, the computer can do nothing. The operating system is built from lots of small programs each of which controls some part of the hardware. Together, these programs allow the operator to use the computer. Operating systems are very complex; some control a simple stand-alone computer, others control whole networks of machines linked together.

Applications

Once the computer has an operating system, you can load applications software to do a particular task such as word processing or payroll.

When you buy an application, you have to choose a version which runs on your particular IT system, including your operating system.

Many applications are considered elsewhere in this course. The main features of the applications are as follows:

- Programs are grouped to form a **package** or suite of programs which together perform a particular function, e.g. invoicing or database management.
- A manufacturer of software will tend to use the same operating methods for all their software, which makes it easier for a user to learn new packages – the emphasis is on **user-friendly** software.
- Most software packages are **menu-driven**; you might select using arrow keys and pressing enter or by pressing the initial letter of your choice (P for print, S for save and so on) or by moving the mouse pointer to your choice and clicking on it.
- DOS-based software is likely to use **functions keys** or **multiple key strokes** to make special things happen; Windows-based software will involve using the **mouse** to click, or double click, **icons**.

- **On-screen help** will be available – so if you get stuck you can press the help key and find out what to do next.

Storage devices

Storage devices are an essential part of an IT system. There are two main types: internal and external devices. The internal devices – within the computer itself – are called **memory** devices. External devices – connected to the computer by cables from the I/O ports – are called **storage** devices.

Three terms are used to describe these device types: auxiliary storage, permanent memory and temporary memory.

- **Auxiliary storage** is a permanent store on a device attached to the IT system, e.g. a disk. Temporary (RAM) and permanent (ROM) stores exist within the computer housing itself. The difference between them is the type of storage used: volatile or non-volatile.
- **Volatile** memory is a form of storage which holds data only while power is supplied. This is therefore a **temporary** store. RAM is a volatile, temporary store for data and programs.
- **Non-volatile** memory keeps its contents even when the system is switched off. This **permanent memory** retains its contents regardless of power supply and cannot be erased or altered. ROM is a non-volatile, permanent store for programs; it is generally used for the operating system of a computer. All auxiliary stores are non-volatile.

RAM

RAM – random access memory – is memory that has the same access time for all locations. Each location holds one byte and is directly addressable. RAM may be either **static**, which holds its memory while there is a power supply, or **dynamic**, which has to be refreshed by reading and rewriting the contents very frequently (about every 2 milliseconds). Dynamic RAM (DRAM) is more widely used than static RAM because it needs less power.

ROM

ROM – read only memory – is memory where the contents may be read, but cannot be written to, by the computer system. This is used for both data and programs.

There are optical ROM systems and semiconductor (integrated circuit) ROM systems. The term ROM is frequently used to mean the (integrated circuit) read only memory used to hold programs and associated data for building into computers.

Software in ROM is fixed during manufacture, but there are other ways of putting programs and data into ROM:

- **PROM** (programmable read only memory) is a type of ROM which is manufactured as an empty storage array and can be permanently programmed by the user later.
- **EPROM** (erasable PROM) is a type of PROM whose data can be erased by a special process (e.g. by exposure to ultraviolet radiation) so new data can be written as if it were a new PROM.

Disk

To use disk storage you need two things:

1. The **device** (the hardware machine to read/write to the disk) which is called the **drive**.
2. The **medium** (the disk on which you read/write from).

A **disk drive** is the device or unit made up of the mechanism that rotates the disks between the read/write heads, and the mechanism that controls these heads. Most disk drives have one set of read/write heads for each surface, which have to be moved to the required track. A disk unit with one set of heads for each disk track is called a **fixed head disk unit**. This arrangement gives much faster access to data on the disk(s) but at increased cost.

A **hard disk drive** uses rigid magnetic disk(s) enclosed in a sealed container. It has the advantage of allowing high recording density because the recording heads can be very close to the magnetic material on the disk. Small hard disk drives, sometimes known as Winchester disks (or drives), are widely used in microcomputer systems as the principle back-up store in addition to one or more floppy disk drives (Figure 3.12).

Floppy disk drives use flexible disks which can be removed from their drives by the user, unlike hard disks which are permanently mounted within the computer.

A **CD-ROM drive** (sometimes called a CD-ROM player) is very similar to an audio compact disk player and is used to read CD-ROM. A CD-ROM jukebox is a CD-ROM drive with a mechanism for automatically changing the current disk for another selected disk; this is similar to the old-fashioned jukebox for playing gramophone records.

Floppy disk drive

Hard disk drive within processor

Figure 3.12 **Floppy and hard disk drives**

A **magnetic disk**, usually made of plastic, is coated with a layer of magnetic material on which data can be stored by magnetically setting the arrangement of the magnetic material. This is done by electromagnetic read/write heads. Disks may have data stored on one side only (single-sided) or on both sides (double-sided). The disk may be rigid (a hard disk), or flexible (a floppy disk). Where a disk drive has multiple disks (a disk pack) these are generally rigid hard disks on a common spindle with read/write heads for each disk. If the disk pack is removable so that it can be exchanged for another complete pack, it is called an exchangeable disk pack.

A **floppy disk** (sometimes called a diskette) is protected by an outer covering which prevents the magnetic coating from being damaged and keeps out dirt. Floppy disks are made to agreed standard designs, and so can be used on any drive designed for the same size disk. The commonest size is $3\frac{1}{2}$ inch, but the earlier $5\frac{1}{4}$ inch standard is also still used (Figure 3.13).

Floppy disks need to have some way of showing where the tracks start. In $5\frac{1}{4}$ inch disks this is done by an index hole – a small hole near

Figure 3.13 **Types of floppy disks and a CD**

the central hole – which lines up with a gap in the casing once every revolution. In $3\frac{1}{2}$ inch disks, it is only possible to fit the disk into the drive in one position.

Purpose of the components

Each of the components discussed so far in this chapter has a specific purpose – a role to play in your use of an IT system.

Data capture

Data capture describes the method used to get data into an IT system. Generally, you use an input device such as a keyboard, a mouse or a sensor. Some special **automated methods** are described here.

A **mark sense reader** is an input device that reads special forms (or cards) by detecting the marks made on the form in predetermined positions. The marks may be handwritten or they may be printed in some way. There are four main types of mark sensing:

1. An **optical mark reader** (OMR) reads marks made in predetermined positions on special forms (or cards) by a light-sensing method; for example, the numbers recorded on a National Lottery entry form or a multiple choice test answer sheet. (See Figure 3.14.)

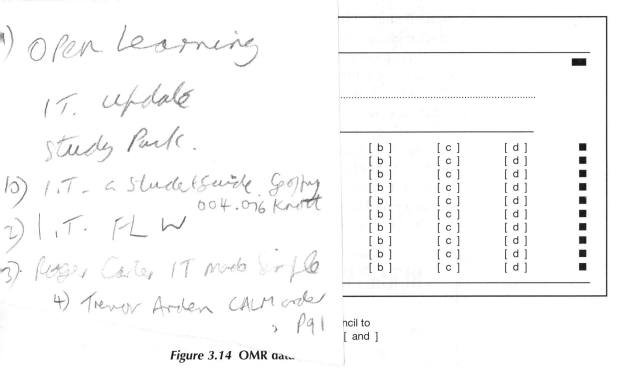

Figure 3.14 OMR data

2. **Magnetic ink character recognition** (MICR) is machine
   recognition of characters printed in magnetic ink. The commonest
   application is the data printed on a cheque; this usually includes
   the cheque number, the branch number and the account number.
   These characters are readable by both machines and humans. (See
   Figure 3.15.)

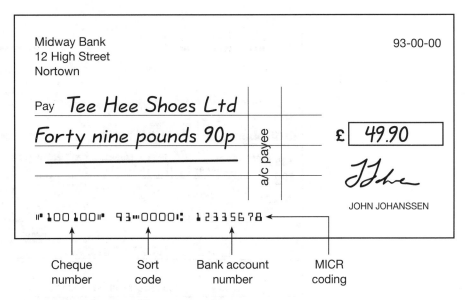

Figure 3.15 **Cheque with MICR markings**

3. **Optical character recognition** (OCR) is machine recognition of printed characters by light-sensing methods, e.g. the reading of typed postcodes when mail is automatically sorted or the machine-readable section of a European Community passport. (See Figure 3.16.)

4. A **bar code reader** or scanner is used to read information in bar code form. Sometimes the reader is built into equipment such as a supermarket checkout terminal. This form of reader shines laser light onto the object being scanned and interprets the patterns reflected by the bar code. An alternative form is a handheld device, called a wand (Figure 3.17); this also works by sensing light reflected by the bar code.

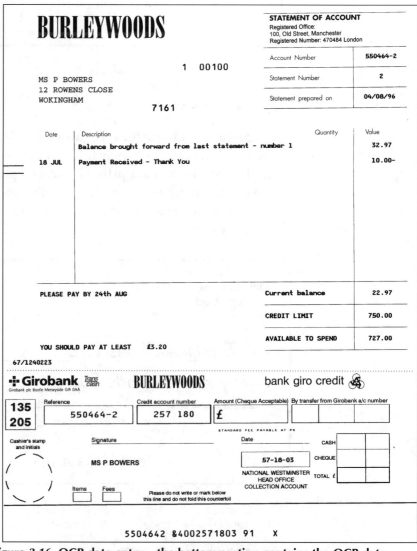

Figure 3.16 **OCR data entry – the bottom section contains the OCR data**

These four methods provide quick ways of capturing data, and can reduce the number of errors made. They do involve some extra work, e.g. setting up bar codes initially, but the whole process then becomes automatic, saving both time and money.

Figure 3.17 **Typical bar code scanner used in libraries**

Data display

Data display is the purpose of most output devices – the screen and printer in particular.

Display of data is an important part of data entry; it shows the operator what has been keyed, so it can be checked against the original input document. This is called **screen verification**.

Display is also necessary for **interaction** between the operator and the IT system. **Menus** are displayed and the operator makes a choice; **messages** are displayed if the operator does something strange, or if the equipment does not perform as expected.

Data processing

Data processing is the main objective of an IT system and the most important part of the hardware, but there is little to say about it. Programs are stored within the computer, they are run by the processor and data is processed to give the result required. The processing may involve calculations, sorting records into an order or searching for a particular record. All these activities are part of data processing.

If the computer has a large memory capacity (RAM and ROM) and a high-speed processor, you will have a powerful IT system to process your data.

Printed output

Printed output is often a main product of an IT system: invoices, payslips, management reports, letters to clients and so on. But printed output has other uses:

- Printed output – called **hardcopy** – is necessary to keep a permanent record of data that you no longer need to keep on the IT system. This is called **archiving**.
- You may also need a hardcopy of data so that you can take it away from the computer area and study it, or pass it on to someone else. This may be more suitable than giving them a copy of the data on disk.
- When interrogating a database, the number of matches may be one or two, and you could copy this information from the screen, or just remember it. If the query resulted in two hundred matches, it would make more sense to have a printout of the records.

Printed output can be produced on any type of printer: dot matrix, daisy wheel, ink jet or laser. The type of printer used depends on the quality of output required, the speed of printing needed and the cost.

Storage

Storage is carried out by internal memory (RAM or ROM) or external storage devices (disk or tape).

The **auxiliary store** – sometimes called secondary storage or **backing store** – provides long-term storage on disk or tape. This store allows you to access datafiles which are much larger than the capacity of your computer memory and also allows data and programs to be moved from one computer to another. When you **back-up** your datafiles you do so onto a backing store.

Some internal storage must be **permanent** – this holds the operating system, which you need on start-up. The information cannot be changed, and is not lost when the power is turned off. This storage is read only memory (ROM).

Some internal storage is **temporary** – this holds data which is used during the running of your programs, and which may change. This storage is random access memory (RAM).

System operation

The IT system is controlled by its operating system. This is a program resident in the computer (usually, at least in part, in ROM) which controls all the functions of the IT system.

These are the main functions of an operating system:

- **Start-up** – checking that all the peripherals are working and properly connected.
- **Security** – logging on procedures, controlling user access, checking passwords.
- **Communication** – receiving commands from the user (e.g. from the keyboard), displaying messages to the user (e.g. on the screen).
- **Control of peripherals** – for instance sending data to a printer and communicating with the printer so that all data is printed, even though the printer prints more slowly than the computer sends the data to it.
- **Control of memory** – keeping track of what is held on a disk by updating the disk directory.
- **Error control** – checking data on entry and displaying messages if anything is not okay, e.g. a letter keyed into a numeric field.

Process data

Data is processed by the CPU (central processing unit). The CPU has many important functions:

- It controls the running of software programs.
- It controls the movement of data to and from peripherals.
- It does all calculations and all tests, and makes all decisions.
- It controls the timing of the machine.

Find required data and use an IT system

To demonstrate that you can use an IT system, you must prove that you can find data already stored within it. To do this you must know where to look for the information, what instructions (or commands) to use and how to say what it is that you want.

Looking in the right directory

All data is stored in datafiles, and these are stored in directories.

Directories are like filing cabinets. You might keep all correspondence files on customers with names starting with the letters A to D in one drawer, the ones for customers E to K in another drawer, and so on.

Each directory can also be split into sub-directories, and the sub-directories can be split still further as shown in Figure 3.18.

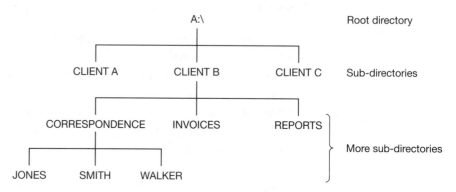

Figure 3.18 **Example directory structure**

It makes sense to decide where to store your datafiles, before you have too many in one directory. There may be a limit to the number of files in any one directory; also each name has to be unique within that directory.

ACTIVITY 3.6

Produce a printout of the datafiles in one of your directories.

Looking for files with a given name

In IT systems, datafiles created in one application have a special name ending (called a **file extension**) which allows the application software to recognise the file next time you want to access it. For example, this book has been written using a word processing package which uses the '.DOC' file extension.

ACTIVITY 3.7

Make a list of the file extensions used by the packages on your IT system.

File extensions are important. If you want to transfer data from one package to another, the formats of the datafiles must be compatible. Knowing the file extension will allow you to check in the software manual whether this type of file can be **imported**. Importing files (rather than just retrieving them) involves a translation process. The same process (but in reverse) happens when you **export** datafiles for use in another software application.

Each datafile also has a name (called its **filename**) chosen by you. It is important to choose names which are meaningful. Then, next time you see the name on the directory list, you will remember what data is in that file.

The **pathname** of a file is the combination of

- the drive letter (which disk drive you have stored the data on)
- the directory name
- any sub-directory names
- the filename
- the file extension

You need to know all these before you can locate a datafile! This chapter is stored on a floppy disk. Its pathname is A:\GNVQ\BOOK\CH3.DOC. The backward slashes (\) separate the different parts of the pathname.

ACTIVITY 3.8

Write down the pathnames of three different datafiles to which you have access.

Searching for data which meets specified criteria

Having found the correct datafile, you will probably want to look at a particular record or group of records.

If a datafile relates to all the people employed by a company, then this datafile is separated into many records, each one related to one particular employee. Each record may have details of the employee, such as:

- name
- address
- job title

These details are stored in separate fields within the record, one field for name, one field for address and so on.

Each record is the same 'shape', that is, it has the same fields. It is easier to imagine this, if you draw a table as shown in Figure 3.9.

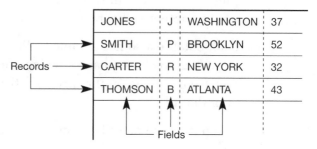

Figure 3.19 **A datafile, split into records and fields**

To find information about a particular employee, you must know something about him or her which will uniquely identify the record. This is called the **key**. Usually, one data item is used as a **key field**. In the case of the employee file, it will probably be an employee number.

ACTIVITY 3.9

What would you expect the key field to be in a datafile held by a bank about each of its customers? Think of three more datafiles and suggest what information might be kept in each record, and what field might be the key field. For example, think about data held by libraries, electricity companies and schools or colleges.

Once you know which record (or group of records) you want to access, you need to enter a command which will make the software search for that data. Exactly how you do this will depend on the software package you are using. Some use a Find command, others use Select. Some offer you a blank record and ask you to fill in the data items you want to match.

ACTIVITY 3.10

Investigate how you find particular records within your software package. Write down an explanation that would help someone who has never used this package before.

Most software packages will allow you to **search on a match**. This means you can find a record which has a data item which exactly matches a data value that you key in. For example, you may match on CUST_NAME = "SMITH" and get a printout of all customers whose surname is Smith. CUST_NAME is the **field title**. The computer will look at every record, and in particular at the data in the field called CUST_NAME. If the data in the field matches, then that record is selected for printing.

You may also want to **search on a range**. For this, you might use a command including the test: PRICE > 100. This might find all records of products which have a sales price greater than £100. You might need to write more complicated instructions which ask for records **within a range**.

ACTIVITY 3.11

Find out what commands you should use to find particular records on a datafile. Write down the command you would use to find a matching record. Write down the command you would use to find a range of records. Use these commands to produce printouts of the data you wanted from the datafile.

If you are not quite sure about how to spell, for instance, a person's surname you can use a **wildcard search**. For example, if you search on CUST_NAME = "SM*", you will be given records for people with surnames Smith, Smithson, Smythe – anyone whose surname starts with 'Sm'.

ACTIVITY 3.12

Find out what wildcard features are available on your software packages. Write down how you would use these features and explain what effect they would have. Produce a printout of data to support your notes.

Use an IT system

You must demonstrate that you can use an IT system. There will be lots of opportunity to do this in other units, and you may use the evidence from those units to support this element. You have to demonstrate that you can:

- input data
- manipulate data
- output data
- store data
- back-up data

You should already know what is meant by input, output and store data.

ACTIVITY 3.13

Write down the instructions you would use to input, output and store data on a software package of your own choice.

Manipulating data involves **editing** the data, that is, changing it in some way. Usually this is to correct an earlier error – a miskeyed name – or to bring the data up-to-date, e.g. if someone moves house and their address details have to be changed.

There are three types of editing: **inserting** new or additional data, **amending** existing data and **deleting** existing data. This may affect data within one record or several records within a datafile.

ACTIVITY 3.14

Produce two printouts of a group of data records, one before editing and one after editing, to prove you have edited these records. Include at least one insert, one amend and one delete in your editing. Explain what key depressions you used to achieve each edit.

To **back-up** data involves saving a copy of the data to a safe place. This should be done regularly, e.g. daily, so that if there is any problem you can retrieve your data from the back-up copy. Back-up copies are usually stored away from the IT system, e.g. in a fireproof safe.

ACTIVITY 3.15

Write down the instructions you would need to use to take a back-up copy of a datafile. Write down how you would retrieve the data in that file should your main copy of the data develop a fault.

Meeting requirements

It is important, when retrieving data from a datafile, that you meet the requirements set. A printout is very useful if:

- it includes all the data required
- the data records are in the order required
- the layout is easy to understand

A printout is not so useful if:

- there is no heading on the report, or no column titles, or no date
- some of the data fields are missing
- not all the required records have been printed

The three factors which decide whether you have produced output in a way that meets requirements are:

- **Fitness for purpose** – does the data answer whatever questions were being asked?
- **Clarity** – is the layout easy to read? Is the report properly headed?
- **Accuracy** – have you included the correct records and the correct fields?

If you meet all three of these, then you have met the performance criteria in full.

The evidence indicators

To prove you have covered the material of this element you need to produce a list:

- identifying the components of an IT system
- describing the purpose of the components of an IT system
- identifying the reasons for using IT

You also need to provide a demonstration of your:

- finding the data required for a task
- using an IT system
- presenting output in a way which meets requirements

Wordsearch 1

These words have been used in Unit 1, find them in the wordsearch below.

AUXILIARY   EFT   PRINTER   TELETEXT
BACS   FACTORY   RADIO   TELEPHONE
BANK   FAX   RAM   TELEVISION
CAPTURE   GRAPHIC   ROM   TEMPORARY
DATA   INVOICING   SENSOR   VDU
DATABASE   KEYBOARD   SHOP   WORD PROCESSING
DIRECT DEBIT   MOUSE   SOFTWARE
DISPLAY   NETWORK   SPREADSHEET
DTP   PERMANENT   STOCK CONTROL

D	I	S	P	L	A	Y	R	A	R	O	P	M	E	T
R	N	P	E	O	M	O	R	R	R	R	P	R	K	E
A	V	R	F	R	M	S	A	O	I	I	A	P	N	L
O	O	E	X	T	U	D	E	N	T	W	A	O	A	E
B	I	A	N	N	I	T	T	S	T	C	H	H	B	T
Y	C	D	O	O	I	E	P	F	A	P	A	S	B	E
E	I	S	I	C	R	O	O	A	E	B	K	F	A	X
K	N	H	S	K	T	S	T	L	C	S	A	V	T	T
S	G	E	I	C	I	S	E	A	T	A	D	T	O	P
R	B	E	V	O	S	T	R	E	S	U	O	M	A	T
O	A	T	E	T	I	B	E	D	T	C	E	R	I	D
S	C	M	L	S	T	N	E	N	A	M	R	E	P	J
N	S	A	E	T	Y	R	A	I	L	I	X	U	A	T
E	N	E	T	W	O	R	K	G	R	A	P	H	I	C
S	G	N	I	S	S	E	C	O	R	P	D	R	O	W

Sample test for Unit 1

Check that you have understood the material of this unit, by doing these sample external test questions.

These questions have been based on questions set by two of the three awarding bodies for GNVQ: RSA and City & Guilds. The questions set by BTEC are similar.

Each question offers four options, but only one of them is correct. At the end of this book, the correct answers are given.

Read each question very carefully before making your decision.

Question 1 In a grocery shop, every product has a coded label which can be read at the point of sale. This coded label is called:

  a   a switch code
  b   a stock control number
  c   an employee code
  d   a bar code

Question 2 The computer system in a chain of supermarkets keeps a record of every item sold and re-orders when necessary. This process is called:

  a   automatic billing
  b   payroll
  c   stock control
  d   bar code scanning

Question 3 Which ONE of the following is the benefit of introducing an electronic point-of-sale (EPOS) system into a supermarket store?

  a   customers are served more quickly
  b   more goods are bought
  c   prices are kept down
  d   stock never runs out

Question 4 A manufacturer of saloon cars has replaced the work done by people with work done by machines in most parts of the factory. This is called:

  a   systematic production
  b   automated production
  c   manual production
  d   phased production

Question 5 Many organisations use a computer system to calculate wages. This procedure uses:

    a   an invoicing system
    b   a product ordering system
    c   a payroll system
    d   a stock control system

Question 6 Which ONE of the following is a benefit of introducing automated production into a factory?

    a   increased availability of information
    b   increased human error
    c   increased accuracy in the production process
    d   increased cost of production

Question 7 A person buys clothes in a department store and pays by debit card. This method of payment is called:

    a   standing order
    b   electronic funds transfer at point-of-sale (EFTPOS)
    c   bankers automated clearing system (BACS)
    d   direct debit

Question 8 A customer instructs the telephone company to collect payment for telephone bills from his bank account. This payment method is called:

    a   clearing a cheque
    b   electronic point-of-sale (EPOS)
    c   bankers automated clearing system (BACS)
    d   direct debit

Question 9 Which ONE of the following is a limitation for a bank when using IT systems?

    a   increased accuracy
    b   reduced impact on the environment
    c   risk of loss of information
    d   increased speed of transactions

Question 10 A travel agent uses a computerised system to check the availability of aeroplane tickets. This is called:

    a   a booking system
    b   a local viewdata system
    c   a teletext system
    d   a CD-ROM system

Question 11   Which ONE of the following would be offered on an entertainment booking system?

    a   rail tickets
    b   theatre tickets
    c   dentist's appointment
    d   meeting with an accountant

Question 12   A person planning to see a show many miles from home appreciates the speed of booking a ticket using a booking agency IT system. ONE limitation of using a booking agency IT system is:

    a   loss of information can result from machine failure
    b   the agency checks availability quickly
    c   the agency's fee is very low
    d   up-to-date information is available

Question 13   A salesperson urgently needs to send a hardcopy of a three-page A4 document to a client 200 miles away. Which ONE of the following types of electronic communication is used?

    a   teletext
    b   fax (facsimile)
    c   telephone
    d   television

Question 14   An organisation for the deaf wishes to tell its members about a special meeting using its bulletin board. This information can be accessed by using a handheld TV remote control and uses:

    a   a fax (facsimile)
    b   teletext
    c   telephone lines
    d   computer networks

Question 15   A firm promotes a new product to its customers through a computer communication network. This uses:

    a   fax (facsimile)
    b   telephone
    c   radio
    d   electronic mail

Question 16   Which ONE of the following would be chosen for an office that needs a software package to produce text only documents?

a   a spreadsheet package
b   a database package
c   a word processing package
d   a graphics package

Question 17   Which ONE of the following software packages is best suited to producing illustrations for a monthly magazine?

a   a graphics package
b   a database package
c   a word processing package
d   a spreadsheet package

Question 18   Which ONE of the following packages best allows the calculation of income and expenses?

a   a desktop publishing (DTP) package
b   a spreadsheet package
c   a graphics package
d   a database package

Question 19   A large insurance company has installed a new spreadsheet package. Which ONE of the following would be the main problem faced by the users?

a   more monitors would be needed
b   staff would need to be trained
c   work would be speeded up
d   efficiency would be improved

Question 20   The owner of a small florist's shop decides against purchasing a computer system to calculate the yearly accounts. This is because:

a   there are only small amounts of data to be processed
b   most florists do not have a computer system
c   a spreadsheet package only produces tables
d   fewer mistakes will be made in the accounts

Question 21   The market research department of a company handles large amounts of data. The greatest benefit of using a database to store this data is:

a   the space required for storing data is increased
b   the initial development time is long
c   the data can be accessed quickly
d   the data can be held securely

Question 22   Refer to Figure T1.1. The component marked X is a:

    a   printer
    b   keyboard
    c   mouse
    d   disk drive

Figure T1.1

Question 23   Refer to Figure T1.1. The component marked Y is a:

    a   VDU
    b   mouse
    c   main processor unit
    d   storage device

Question 24   Refer to Figure T1.1. The component marked Z is a:

    a   main processor unit
    b   software application
    c   keyboard
    d   mouse

Question 25   Which ONE of the following can only be used for data capture?

a   ROM
b   VDU
c   sensor
d   printer

Question 26   Which ONE of the following devices is used only for output?

a   printer
b   mouse
c   VDU
d   disk

Question 27   Which ONE of the following is a device in which data processing takes place?

a   word processing package
b   plotter
c   main processor unit
d   storage device

Question 28   Which ONE of the following is a temporary storage device?

a   ROM
b   RAM
c   disk
d   CD-ROM

Question 29   At the end of each day an IT manager makes a back-up copy of all files and this is stored separately. This copy is called:

a   data capture
b   temporary storage
c   permanent storage
d   data display

Question 30   A weather station measures wind speed and rainfall every day. The data is then entered into a computer. This process is called:

a   data display
b   data capture
c   sorting data
d   backing-up data

Question 31   Data taken from a survey of radio listeners is analysed so that the producer can see how many like or dislike the programme. This analysis is called:

a   data storage
b   backing-up data
c   processing data
d   data input

Using information technology

This section covers the material needed for Unit 2: Using information technology.

There are four chapters which match the four elements in Unit 2:

- Chapter 4 covers Element 2.1: Process documents
- Chapter 5 covers Element 2.2: Process graphic images
- Chapter 6 covers Element 2.3: Process numerical information
- Chapter 7 covers Element 2.4: Process structured data

Every chapter in this section involves lots of practical work. None of the chapters tries to teach you how to use a particular software package. Instead, we concentrate on explaining the terms used, and why things are done in a certain way.

You will need to try as many different software packages as your centre allows. Then you will be better prepared for whatever software you may find at work.

External test

For this unit, the external test has approximately 30 multiple choice questions. A complete test covering the whole unit is given at the end of Chapter 7; the answers to this test are given at the end of the book.

4 Process documents

Introduction

This chapter covers the material needed for Element 2.1: Process documents.

The performance criteria state that the student must:

1. Create appropriate document **layouts** for given tasks.
2. Enter and combine **data**.
3. **Edit documents** and **check accuracy** of data.
4. Save regularly using suitable **filenames**.
5. Output documents.

The knowledge range

To meet the performance criteria, you *must* cover the range. The words shown in bold in the performance criteria above highlight the skills and knowledge you will need, and so we will now consider each of these in turn.

Layouts

Document layouts depend on:

- the information within the document
- what you will use the document for

Letters have a different layout from memos. Newspapers use several columns; text books may only have a single column. Figure 4.1 shows several different document layouts.

Figure 4.1 Document layout examples

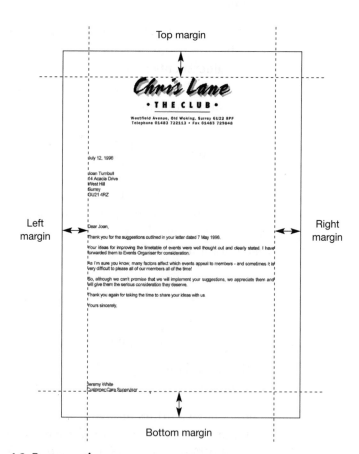

Figure 4.2 Page margins

ACTIVITY 4.1

Collect at least four different documents, showing a range of layouts. Write a paragraph on each explaining its use. Store this work in your portfolio folder.

Margins

Each page has *four* margins: top, bottom, left and right. Figure 4.2 shows these margins on a sample document. Documents are usually filed, so they need a left margin wide enough for hole punching.

ACTIVITY 4.2

Using the documents collected in Activity 4.1, identify the margins used. Are the margins wide enough for filing? What is the standard size for the left margin? How much margin is needed on the right-hand side?

Justification

Text can be arranged on a page in a number of ways.

Full justification is used for most business documents. It results in both edges of text being straight (Figure 4.3(a)). To achieve this effect, the software adds extra space between pairs of words so that the words on each line fill that line completely. The spaces you key in are called **hard** spaces; the spaces inserted by the software are called **soft** spaces. Full justification is used in newspaper columns and text books. Sometimes it is referred to as **justification on**; **justification off** would mean left justified only.

Left justification means the left-hand edge of the text will be straight but the right-hand edge will be ragged (Figure 4.3(b)).

Right justification means that the right-hand edge will be straight but the left-hand edge of the text will be ragged (Figure 4.3(c)). This would look strange on normal text, e.g. in a letter, but is often used when text and graphics are incorporated in the same document. This style may also be used to create special effects.

Centred text appears in the centre of each line (Figure 4.3(d)). Centred text is often used on menus, programmes or front pages of reports.

Ut wisi enim ad minim veniam, quis nostrud exerci tation ullamcorper suscipit lobortis nisl ut aliquip ex ae commodo consequat. Duis autem vel eum iriure dolor in hendrerit in vulputate velit esse molestie consequat. (a)

Ut wisi enim ad minim veniam, quis nostrud exerci tation ullamcorper suscipit lobortis nisl ut aliquip ex ae commodo consequat. Duis autem vel eum iriure dolor in hendrerit in vulputate velit esse molestie consequat. (b)

Ut wisi enim ad minim veniam, quis nostrud exerci tation ullamcorper suscipit lobortis nisl ut aliquip ex ae commodo consequat. Duis autem vel eum iriure dolor in hendrerit in vulputate velit esse molestie consequat. (c)

Ut wisi enim ad minim veniam, quis nostrud exerci tation ullamcorper suscipit lobortis nisl ut aliquip ex ae commodo consequat. Duis autem vel eum iriure dolor in hendrerit in vulputate velit esse molestie consequat. (d)

Figure 4.3 **Different types of justifications: (a) full; (b) left; (c) right; (d) centred**

No indentation
{
Lorem ipsum dolor sit amet, consecteturer apipiscin elit, sed diam nonummy nibh euismod tincidunt ut laoreet dolore magna aliquam erat volutpat.
Duis autem vel eum iriure dolor in hendrerit in vulputate velit esse molestie consequat. Vel illum dolore eu feugiat nulla facilisis at vero eros et accumsan et iusto odio dignissim qui blandit praesent luptatum incidunt.

Indented for each new paragraph
{
Lorem ipsum dolor sit amet, consecteturer apipiscin elit, sed diam nonummy nibh euismod tincidunt ut laoreet dolore magna aliquam erat volutpat.
Duis autem vel eum iriure dolor in hendrerit in vulputate velit esse molestie consequat. Vel illum dolore eu feugiat nulla facilisis at vero eros et accumsan et iusto odio dignissim qui blandit praesent luptatum incidunt.

Text indented for display purposes
{
Lorem ipsum dolor sit amet, consecteturer apipiscin elit, sed diam nonummy nibh euismod tincidunt ut laoreet dolore magna aliquam erat volutpat.
Duis autem vel eum iriure dolor in hendrerit in vulputate velit esse molestie consequat. Vel illum dolore eu feugiat nulla facilisis at vero eros et accumsan et iusto odio dignissim qui blandit praesent luptatum incidunt.

Hanging indent used for lists
{
Lorem ipsum dolor sit amet, consecteturer apipiscin elit, sed diam nonummy nibh euismod tincidunt ut laoreet dolore magna aliquam erat volutpat.

1. Duis autem vel eum iriure dolor in hendrerit in vulputate velit esse molestie consequat.
2. Vel illum dolore eu feugiat nulla facilisis at vero eros et accumsan et iusto odio dignissim qui blandit praesent luptatum incidunt.

Figure 4.4 **Using indentation and tabulation to format lists**

ACTIVITY 4.3

Collect examples of all four types of justification. Make notes on why they are used and store this work in your portfolio folder.

Indents and tabs

The **indent** is the amount of space between the margin and the start of the text. Text can be indented on either side, on both sides or not at all. Figure 4.4 shows several examples of indentation.

Hanging indents give the effect of a list. The list can be numbered, or bullet points may be used instead. Figure 4.5 shows both types of list.

To create the effect of columns, we use **tabulation** (tabs). The tab key is pressed to make the cursor jump to the next tab position. Figure 4.5 also shows how setting tab positions can produce indented lists.

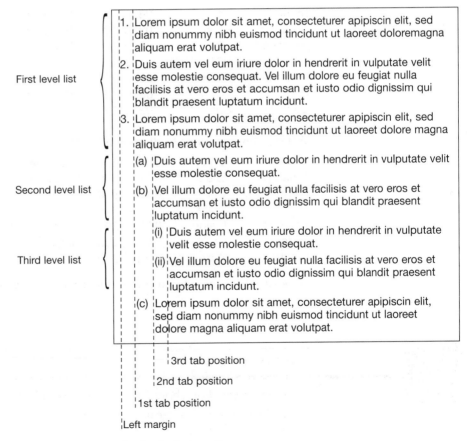

Figure 4.5 **Using tabs for laying out lists**

The benefit of using tabs rather than hard spaces is that you can change tab positions very easily. Depending on the software you are using, you may set up a **ruler** with tab positions marked. If you move the tab position of the ruler, all text controlled by that ruler will move to the new positions.

Figure 4.6 shows how changing the ruler can change the presentation of text in columns.

No tabs set

MondayChris0830–1400Suzanne1400–1730
TuesdayElaine0830–1300Suzanne1300–1730
WednesdayChris0830–1230Elaine1230–1730
Katie0845–1345
ThursdayElaine0830–1300Suzanne1300–1730
FridayChris0830–1300Suzanne1330–1730
SaturdaySuzanne0900–1230

Tabs set at regular intervals

Monday	Chris	0830–1400	Suzanne	1400–1730
Tuesday	Elaine	0830–1300	Suzanne	1300–1730
Wednesday	Chris	0830–1230	Elaine	1230–1730
	Katie	0845–1345		
Thursday	Elaine	0830–1300	Suzanne	1300–1730
Friday	Chris	0830–1300	Suzanne	1330–1730
Saturday	Suzanhe	0900–1230		

Tab positions moved to display all data clearly

Monday	Chris	0830–1400	Suzanne	1400–1730
Tuesday	Elaine	0830–1300	Suzanne	1300–1730
Wednesday	Chris	0830–1230	Elaine	1230–1730
	Katie	0845–1345		
Thursday	Elaine	0830–1300	Suzanne	1300–1730
Friday	Chris	0830–1300	Suzanne	1330–1730
Saturday	Suzanne	0900–1230		

Figure 4.6 **Using the ruler to control the format of columns**

ACTIVITY 4.4

Collect examples to show different types of indentation and the use of tabs. Make notes on their use and store your work in your portfolio folder.

Line spacing

'Normal text' has **single line spacing**. It is possible, though, to use different line spacing.

Double line spacing has an extra line of space after each line of text. This is useful if your work is still in draft form and you might need space to write in corrections. Figure 4.7 shows examples of both spacings.

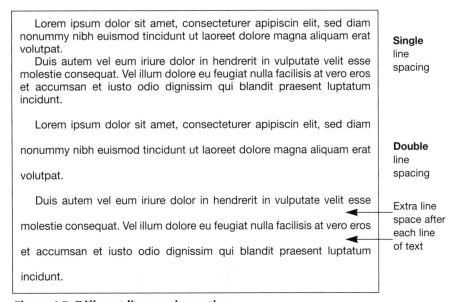

Figure 4.7 Different line spacing options

ACTIVITY 4.5

Produce one sheet of text showing both single and double line spacing. Make notes on the word processing package you used and how you achieved this effect. Check whether other word processing packages offer this facility, and make notes on how it is done. Do all word processing packages use the same method?

Font styles and sizes

The term **type** describes all the printed letters (a–z, A–Z), numbers (0–9) and other characters and symbols (!, ", £, $, %, etc.). Figure 4.8 shows a few examples of different typefaces.

Sanserif	Serif
Helvetica	Book Antiqua
Antique Olive	Century Schoolbook
Futura	Courier New
Letter Gothic	Times New Roman

Figure 4.8 **Serif and sanserif typefaces**

There are two 'families' of typeface: those with **serifs** and those without (known as **sanserif**). Figure 4.8 shows both types. Sanserif looks 'cleaner' and is often used for headlines. Serif fonts are used for normal reading text.

A **font** is a typeface of a particular **size** and **attribute**. For example, 12 pt Times Roman is one font, 8 pt Times Roman is another. The abbreviation 'pt' stands for 'point'. **Point size** is a measure of the vertical dimension of a font. Figure 4.9 shows the same typeface at different point sizes.

Helvetica	8pt	8 points
Helvetica	10pt	
Helvetica	12pt	
Helvetica	14pt	14 points
Helvetica	20pt	
Helvetica	24pt	24 points

Figure 4.9 **Different point sizes**

Pitch refers to the number of characters printed in a horizontal inch.

To **highlight** certain words in a passage you can use fonts with special **attributes**. You can also use single or double underlining to make important words stand out. Figure 4.10 shows some examples of highlighting important text.

ACTIVITY 4.6

Find out which typefaces are available on a particular word processing package. Print out samples and label them with the font name and point size. Include at least one serif and one sanserif typeface. File this information in your portfolio folder.

Strawberry Flan

Cream 1 ounce unsalted butter with 1 tablespoon of castor sugar.
Beat in 4 ounces of cream cheese.
Add 1 tablespoon of double cream and beat well until smooth.
Make a pastry case (8") and bake blind.
Smooth the beaten mixture over the base of the cooked pastry and top with strawberries.
Warm 2 tablespoons of redcurrant jelly with 1 tablespoon of lemon juice. When melted, cool and spoon glaze over the strawberries.
Serve with single cream.

No highlighting

Strawberry Flan

Cream 1 ounce **unsalted butter** with 1 tablespoon of **castor sugar.**
Beat in 4 ounces of **cream cheese.**
Add 1 tablespoon of **double cream** and beat well until smooth.
Make a **pastry case** (8") and bake blind.
Smooth the beaten mixture over the base of the cooked pastry and top with **strawberries.**
Warm 2 tablespoons of **redcurrant jelly** with 1 tablespoon of **lemon juice.** When melted, cool and spoon glaze over the strawberries.
Serve with **single cream.**

Using bold

Strawberry Flan

Cream 1 ounce *unsalted butter* with 1 tablespoon of *castor sugar.*
Beat in 4 ounces of *cream cheese.*
Add 1 tablespoon of *double cream* and beat well until smooth.
Make a *pastry case* (8") and bake blind.
Smooth the beaten mixture over the base of the cooked pastry and top with *strawberries.*
Warm 2 tablespoons of *redcurrant jelly* with 1 tablespoon of *lemon juice.* When melted, cool and spoon glaze over the strawberries.
Serve with *single cream.*

Using italic

Strawberry Flan

Cream 1 ounce `unsalted butter` with 1 tablespoon of `castor sugar.`
Beat in 4 ounces of `cream cheese.`
Add 1 tablespoon of `double cream` and beat well until smooth.
Make a `pastry case` (8") and bake blind.
Smooth the beaten mixture over the base of the cooked pastry and top with `strawberries.`
Warm 2 tablespoons of `redcurrant jelly` with 1 tablespoon of `lemon juice.` When melted, cool and spoon glaze over the strawberries.
Serve with `single cream.`

Using a different font

Figure 4.10 **Highlighting text using different font attributes**

Page numbering

When you produce a document which is longer than three or four pages it is usual to number the pages.

Page numbering usually appears at the top (in the 'header') or at the bottom (in the 'footer') of each page. Examples are shown in Figure 4.11.

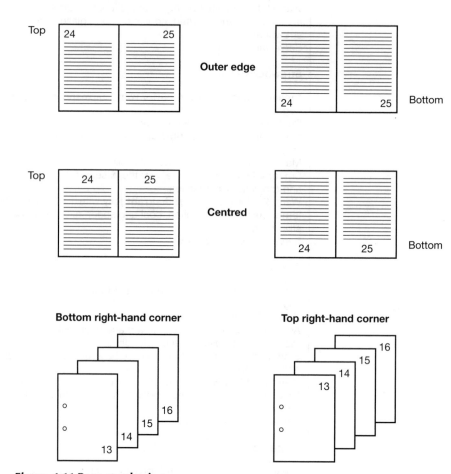

Figure 4.11 **Page numbering**

Some word processing packages allow you to include the chapter number as part of the page number.

Usually page numbers start at 1, and go up by one for each new page: 1, 2, 3, 4 and so on. This is called **Arabic numbering**. Some word processing packages allow counting in **Roman numbers**: i, ii, iii, iv, v, vi, and so on.

Page numbering is essential for large books which need a contents page and may include an index (Figure 4.12).

Figure 4.12 **Typical index layout**

Pagination

A text file may be too long to fit on one sheet of paper. If so, the text has to be paginated, that is, broken into pages.

Pagination is done automatically by the software so that no text is lost when printing.

If you want to control pagination you must put a **page break** in to show where you want the new page to start (Figure 4.13).

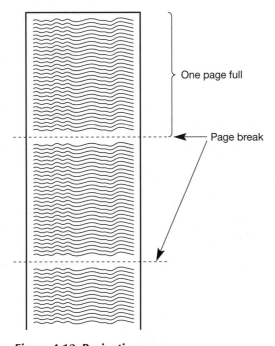

One page full

Page break

Figure 4.13 **Pagination**

ACTIVITY 4.7

Using a document (more than two pages long) place a page break at a suitable point. Include the page number, either in a footer or a header. File a printout of the document in your portfolio folder.

Data

When creating a document, the data may come from:

- your head – you invent the work while you are keying it in
- existing computer files – you may retrieve a file to make some changes
- libraries – graphics particularly are often available in this format

The data may also involve:

- text – words, sentences, paragraphs, headings and so on
- tables – data that appears in columns
- graphics – figures and drawings

Figure 4.14 uses all these sources of data.

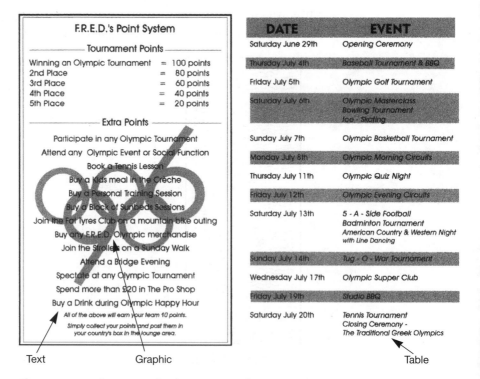

Figure 4.14 **Using more than one source data**

Text, tables and graphics

The data in a document is usually divided into the three types – text, tables and graphics – because different methods are used to enter them on an IT system.

Text is usually keyed in using the keyboard and a word processing or text editing package.

Tables involve a lot of tabulation and so need greater skill from the keyboard operator.

Graphics require drawing skills. They can be drawn on paper and scanned into the IT system. Otherwise, a drawing package is needed, and a mouse is used to draw and edit the image. For those of us who cannot draw, **clip-art** offers us the chance to use the graphics prepared by others. We can edit these to suit our purposes and make them our own, without having any artistic ability.

ACTIVITY 4.8

In the four examples shown in Figure 4.15, decide whether each is text, a table or a graphic.

1. Use one colour of highlighter pen to pick out all the material that you would need to produce using graphics software.
2. Use a different colour highlighter to pick out the tables.

What is left should be only text, that can be keyed in on a keyboard.

Text

Text is simply lots of **characters** – any of the ones on a keyboard plus some more.

These characters are grouped into **words**. The IT systems software – usually a word processing package – recognises a 'word' as a series of characters ending in a space.

The words are grouped into **sentences**. The software recognises a 'sentence' as a series of words ending in a full stop.

The sentences are grouped into **paragraphs**. The software recognises paragraphs as blocks. These are separated by some special character, e.g. a return.

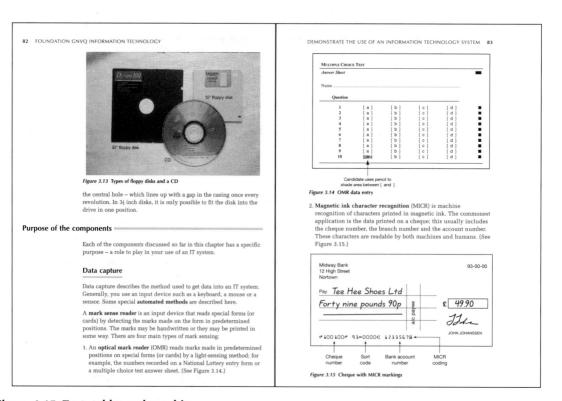

Figure 4.15 **Text, tables and graphics**

Figure 4.16 shows examples of characters, words, sentences and paragraphs.

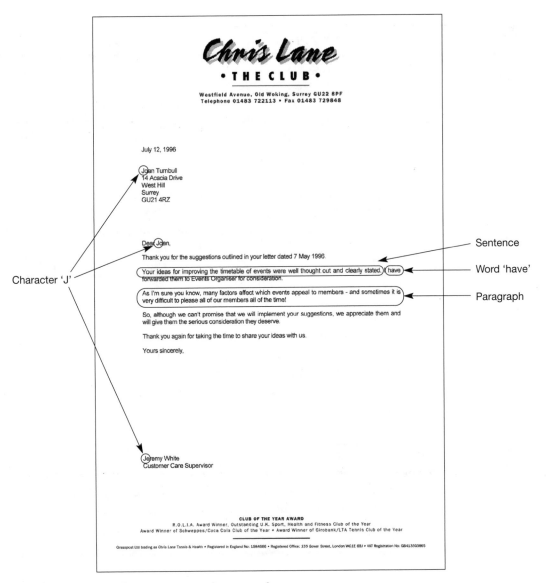

Figure 4.16 **Characters, words, sentences and paragraphs**

When you key in text, as each character is pressed on the keyboard, it appears where the cursor is on the screen and the cursor then moves to the next position.

Most people, when keying in, are busy looking at the keyboard. Keyboard operators who can touch-type will be keeping an eye on the document they are copying – they know which keys their fingers are pressing. You should also try to note what is happening on the screen.

When you have keyed enough to fill one line, the cursor jumps to the next line, so the next word suddenly appears below. This is called **wordwrap**.

ACTIVITY 4.9

First make sure you have justification off. Then key in a couple of sentences – at least enough to fill the width of the screen.

1. Watch the screen as you key in the characters of the word that will not fit onto the first line. When does the word move to the next line?
2. Repeat this with justification on. Can you see what differences this makes?
3. Repeat this but leave out the spaces between the last few words (pretending to make a keying error). What does the software treat as a 'word'? Now put the spaces in where they should go. How does the software react?

WYSIWYG – what you see is what you get
While you are keying in text, some word processing packages display exactly what will appear on paper if you print the document. This is called a **WYSIWYG** display. Earlier and less sophisticated word processing packages simply displayed what you had keyed, using the full screen width.

ACTIVITY 4.10

Load or key in a document and check the screen display. Note the words that appear on the right-hand margin. Print out the document. Is yours a WYSIWYG system?

Most word processing packages without WYSIWYG offer a 'view document' option so you can see what it will look like on paper. Some word processing packages offer a 'repaginate' option. If you repaginate, the word processing package formats the text and works out where the page breaks will be. It shows this on the screen, e.g. by putting a dotted line across the screen.

ACTIVITY 4.11

Using a word processing package without the WYSIWYG feature find out how to use the view option and the repagination option.

Tables

Tables can be produced as tabulated text using a word processing package. The text is arranged in columns to make it easier to understand.

A table has four 'ingredients':

1. a title (and sometimes a number, if you have lots of them)
2. column headings
3. column data
4. footnotes (to say where or how the data was obtained or to explain anything)

To separate those four parts, **rules** (horizontal and vertical lines) are used. An example is shown in Figure 4.17.

To make the data appear in columns, tab jumps are used. Where you put the tab stops on your ruler will depend on how much data there is in each column.

ACTIVITY 4.12

Figure 4.18 shows four different tables.

1. Use one colour of highlighter pen to mark the table titles. Note the different styles used. Which style do you prefer?
2. Use a different colour of highlighter pen to mark the column headings. Again, notice the choice of styles.
3. Use one more colour to highlight any footnotes.

The material you have not highlighted should be the column data. Notice the different types of justification used.

Studio timetable – Mondays from 9th April 1996   } Title

Time	Class	Level	Instructor
9.30–10.30	Total Body Sculpture	Gen	Ali
10.30–11.30	Step and Condition	Int	Ali
1.00–2.00	40 Plus	Gen	Elaine
2.00–2.45	Triple Action	Beg/Int	Kim
6.15–7.00	Hi/Lo Aerobics	Int	Suzy
7.00–8.00	Total Body Sculpture	Gen	Ali
8.00–9.00	Step	Int	Ali

} Column headings } Column data

Class levels are given as a guide only: Gen=general; Beg=beginners; Int=intermediate. Please ask your instructor for harder or easier modifications if required.   } Footnotes

Figure 4.17 **Example table style**

Studio timetable – Mondays from 9th April 1996

Time	Class	Level	Instructor
9.30–10.30	Total Body Sculpture	Gen	Ali
10.30–11.30	Step and Condition	Int	Ali
1.00–2.00	40 Plus	Gen	Elaine
2.00–2.45	Triple Action	Beg/Int	Kim
6.15–7.00	Hi/Lo Aerobics	Int	Suzy
7.00–8.00	Total Body Sculpture	Gen	Ali
8.00–9.00	Step	Int	Ali

Class levels are given as a guide only: Gen=general; Beg=beginners; Int=intermediate. Please ask your instructor for harder or easier modifications if required.

Studio timetable – Mondays from 9th April 1996

Time	Class	Level	Instructor
9.30–10.30	Total Body Sculpture	Gen	Ali
10.30–11.30	Step and Condition	Int	Ali
1.00–2.00	40 Plus	Gen	Elaine
2.00–2.45	Triple Action	Beg/Int	Kim
6.15–7.00	Hi/Lo Aerobics	Int	Suzy
7.00–8.00	Total Body Sculpture	Gen	Ali
8.00–9.00	Step	Int	Ali

Class levels are given as a guide only: Gen=general; Beg=beginners; Int=intermediate. Please ask your instructor for harder or easier modifications if required.

Studio timetable – Mondays from 9th April 1996

Time	Class	Level	Instructor
9.30–10.30	Total Body Sculpture	Gen	Ali
10.30–11.30	Step and Condition	Int	Ali
1.00–2.00	40 Plus	Gen	Elaine
2.00–2.45	Triple Action	Beg/Int	Kim
6.15–7.00	Hi/Lo Aerobics	Int	Suzy
7.00–8.00	Total Body Sculpture	Gen	Ali
8.00–9.00	Step	Int	Ali

Class levels are given as a guide only: Gen=general; Beg=beginners; Int=intermediate. Please ask your instructor for harder or easier modifications if required.

Studio timetable – Mondays from 9th April 1996

Time	Class	Level	Instructor
9.30–10.30	Total Body Sculpture	Gen	Ali
10.30–11.30	Step and Condition	Int	Ali
1.00–2.00	40 Plus	Gen	Elaine
2.00–2.45	Triple Action	Beg/Int	Kim
6.15–7.00	Hi/Lo Aerobics	Int	Suzy
7.00–8.00	Total Body Sculpture	Gen	Ali
8.00–9.00	Step	Int	Ali

Class levels are given as a guide only: Gen=general; Beg=beginners; Int=intermediate. Please ask your instructor for harder or easier modifications if required.

Figure 4.18 **Different table formats**

To make the table title stand out, you can use a special text attribute, e.g. bold. The column headings might be put in italic to show that they are different from the data below. Footnotes might be in a smaller point size so they do not distract the reader.

Tables can also be prepared using a spreadsheet package. Spreadsheets allow the figures within a column or row to be added up, giving a total. There are many other features of spreadsheets which make table production easy. This is covered in Chapter 6.

Graphics

A graphic is any drawing which *cannot* be produced using the usual keyboard characters.

Graphics are often used in documents just to add interest. In *Alice in Wonderland*, Alice complained that a book had no pictures. Nowadays, educational software is offered on CD-ROMs, which come full of graphics, and is thought to be more exciting than text books.

Graphics can be used to give information: 'A picture paints a thousand words.' A pie chart or bar chart showing weather data collected every day for a year will 'say' more than a complicated table of figures (Figure 4.19).

Processing graphic images is covered in detail in Chapter 5.

Sources of data

Data may be used from existing sources (on disk files) or it may be developed during input.

Figure 4.19 **Using graphics**

Existing sources

One of the most useful things about IT systems is the facility for the storage of data. You can key in a letter, save it on a floppy disk and then, another day, retrieve the datafile. No rekeying is necessary – unless you lose the file!

You can retrieve data from your own files, but you may also have access to other sources.

Data developed during input

When starting to write something new, it is sometimes difficult to think of exactly what you want to say. With a word processing package you can key in your first thoughts, knowing that they will not be perfect. You can then review and improve them.

This is called **drafting** (and redrafting!). Figure 4.20 shows one document improving through three drafts.

Often the last thing you think of should appear in the first paragraph.

The original thoughts are your own, but you need to be able to edit documents and turn an early draft into a finished document that is good enough to appear in your portfolio folder.

Version one

With a word processing package, you can ~~make changes and~~ try to improve it so you can just key in the first

things you think of.

but you can review it and

Your first thoughts may not be perfect ~~because~~ when ~~you~~ start to write something new, it is ~~really~~ *sometimes*

ing

difficult to think exactly what you want to say.

Version two

When starting to write something new, it is sometimes difficult to think of exactly what you want to say.

With a word processing package, you can key in ~~the first things you think of.~~

, knowing they will

~~Your first thoughts may~~ not be perfect ~~but~~ you can review it and ~~try to~~ improve it.

Then

Version three

When writing something new, it is sometimes difficult to think of exactly what you want to say. With a word processing package, you can key in your first thoughts, knowing they will not be perfect. Then you can review it and improve it.

Figure 4.20 **Drafting and redrafting**

Editing documents

Before IT systems, computers and word processing packages were invented, typists had to type very carefully. If they made a mistake, they would have to retype a letter all over again.

With a word processing package you can **edit** your document. What does this mean?

- You can change your mind about what you want to say.
- You can think of a better way of saying something.
- You can correct any keying errors.
- You can check your spelling.
- You can make sure the finished document is perfect, before printing a copy on paper.

It was thought that the introduction of word processing packages would create the **paperless office**. Instead users tend to print out many draft copies before they are satisfied with the finished document.

The end result may be better, but we often use a lot of paper in the process.

The paperless office?

Insert and delete

There are three types of editing:

1. **insert** – putting in new characters
2. **amend** – altering what is there already
3. **delete** – removing characters

Let's start with **deleting** text. On most keyboards, there are two delete keys: delete backwards (marked 'backspace' or with a backward-pointing arrow), and delete forward (marked 'delete'). Which one you use will depend on the position of your cursor, because the character deleted will be before or after the cursor depending on which key you press. Figure 4.21 shows the two choices for deleting.

ACTIVITY 4.13

Key in a few words of text.

1. Decide on a word (or some characters) to delete. Position your cursor *before* the text to be deleted, and use the delete key.
2. Choose another word to delete. Position your cursor after the text and use the backspace key. What happened? Did the backspace delete backwards, or did it overwrite the text with spaces?

Deleting forwards	*Deleting backwards*
If you want to delete forwards, position the cursor *before* the character you want to lose.	If you want to delete backwards, position the cursor *after* the character you want to lost.
The cat sat on the m<u>o</u>at.	**The cat sat on the mo<u>a</u>t.**
The cursor will flash before or under the character, shown here underlined.	The cursor will flash before or under the character, shown here underlined.
Then press the delete forward key (the 'Delete' key).	Then press the delete backward key (shown as a backward arrow).
The cat sat on the mat.	**The cat sat on the mat.**

Figure 4.21 Deleting forwards or backwards

While keying in, you may be in one of two modes: insert or overtype. While in **insert** mode everything you key in is inserted. The old text moves to the right and nothing is lost. When you use delete (delete forward) or backspace (delete backward), the text disappears and the space is closed up. The text is **deleted** rather than erased.

In **overtype** mode each character you key in overwrites whatever was there before. This is **erasing** text rather than deleting it.

So, to **insert** text, you need to be in insert mode. To **amend** text, you have two choices:

1. Use **overtype** mode, and key the correct characters *over* the incorrect text.
2. Use **insert** mode, first deleting the old text and then keying in the new text.

There will be a key which allows you to **toggle** between insert and overtype modes.

ACTIVITY 4.14

Key in the following text.

Use your word processing skills to produce documentary evidence for all units in Foundation GNVQ Information Technology. The same evidence can then be used for this as well.

1. **Insert** the word 'unit' after 'this'.
2. **Amend** the words 'Information Technology' to read 'IT'.
3. **Delete** the word 'documentary'.

Copy and move

The 'cut and paste' option available on most word processing packages allows you to copy or move text from one place to another within a document.

First, you must identify the text to be 'cut'. Every word processing package is different, but all have a way of highlighting a piece of text.

You may have to press some keys to tell the computer that you want to cut some text. Then press some more keys – perhaps arrow keys – or use the mouse to highlight the piece of text. Next you press a key (or click the mouse) to tell the computer that you are finished and 'hey presto' the piece of text disappears from the screen.

The text that has been cut is, however, safely stored on the computer's **clipboard** ready for pasting. So you can move the cursor to where the text is to reappear, press a button (or click the mouse) and the text will be inserted.

Figure 4.22 shows the sequence used to cut and paste.

It takes longer to read this section on how to do a cut and paste than it does to actually do it on an IT system!

To copy some text the same sequence is used, except the piece highlighted for moving does not disappear. A copy is saved on the clipboard and can be pasted into the new position.

Using bold and italics

Having produced the 'perfect' text, you need to think about **highlighting** important words or phases. These will then catch the reader's eye.

For simplicity, it is best to stick to only one or two highlighting techniques, as using too many makes a document look cluttered.

Figure 4.23 shows two examples: one shows good highlighting, the other has too much.

Emboldening

Words in **bold** stand out more and will be noticed. You should only use bold for headings or to highlight important words. Figure 4.24 gives two examples of good use of bold.

Here is the original text:

The order is incorrect. 'Any other business' should be *after* 'Agenda items'.

```
AGENDA
Minutes of the last meeting
Matters arising
Any other business
Agenda items
Date of the next meeting
```

First, highlight the text to be moved.

```
AGENDA
Minutes of the last meeting
Matters arising
Any other business
Agenda items
Date of the next meeting
```

Then choose 'cut'. The highlighted text will disappear.

```
AGENDA
Minutes of the last meeting
Matters arising
Agenda items
Date of the next meeting
```

Reposition your cursor (shown underlined) where you would like the text to reappear.

```
AGENDA
Minutes of the last meeting
Matters arising
Agenda items
Date of the next meeting
```

Choose 'paste' and the text will have been 'cut and pasted'.

```
AGENDA
Minutes of the last meeting
Matters arising
Agenda items
Any other business
Date of the next meeting
```

Figure 4.22 **How to 'cut and paste'**

<u>***Using a word processing package***</u>

When starting to **write something new**, it is sometimes difficult to think of exactly what you want to say. With a **word processing package**, you can key in your first thoughts, knowing they will not be perfect. Then you can review it and improve it.

The word processing package also offers a **spelling checker**, a **thesaurus** and a **grammar checker**.

The <u>spelling checker</u> highlights **words not found in the dictionary**. The <u>thesaurus</u> suggests **alternative words to use**. The <u>grammar checker</u> highlights sections of text where **you might have made an error**, e.g. using a *singular* noun with a *plural* verb as in 'The <u>*man are*</u> working' or a *plural* noun with a *singular* verb: 'The <u>*men is*</u> working'.

Too much highlighting

Figure 4.23 **Use of highlighting**

Using a word processing package

When starting to write something *new*, it is sometimes difficult to think of exactly what you want to say. With a **word processing package**, you can key in your first thoughts, knowing they will not be perfect. Then you can review it and improve it.

The word processing package also offers a spelling checker, a thesaurus and a grammar checker.

The **spelling checker** highlights words *not* found in the dictionary. The **thesaurus** suggests alternative words to use. The **grammar checker** highlights sections of text where you might have made an error, e.g. using a *singular noun* with a <u>plural verb</u> as in 'The *man* <u>are</u> working' or a *plural noun* with a <u>singular verb</u>: 'The *men* <u>is</u> working'.

Good use of highlighting

The three main **application packages** are:

1. **Word processing packages** which allow you to create documents, amend them, save them and print them out.
2. **Spreadsheet packages** which allow you to process numerical data, print out spreadsheets and charts such as pie charts and bar charts to illustrate the data.
3. **Database packages** which allow you to process related data such as the names and addresses of all your contacts. This data can be sorted into an order, queries made on the data and reports produced.

Most **word processing packages** offer tools such as a spelling checker, a thesaurus and a grammar checker.

The **spelling checker** highlights words not found in the dictionary.

The **thesaurus** suggests alternative words to use.

The **grammar checker** highlights sections of text where you might have made an error.

Figure 4.24 **Two good examples of the use of bold**

Italicising

Italics can be used for headings but it is better used to stress words. If one word in a sentence is important for the sense of what you are saying – and if the reader might miss the importance otherwise – use italics.

Here are two examples:

- In the event of fire, do *not* use the lifts.
- The cost is £25 *plus* VAT.

If your word processor cannot produce italics, use underlining instead.

ACTIVITY 4.15

Find some more examples – in a book or a magazine – where highlighting has been used to stress a single word within a sentence. Do you agree with the need to stress that word? Write down two examples which show good examples of using italics to stress a word, and file this in your portfolio.

Accuracy

Checking accuracy is an important part of document production. A document written by you and given to someone else will make an impression on them. If it is your CV (see Chapter 10), how well you have presented the information can make the difference between being invited for an interview or not.

Checking your own work is very difficult. Your mind reads what it thinks you have written. If possible, ask someone else to check through your wording. If they have queries, you can alter the wording *before* sending the finished document.

Two methods of checking accuracy are:

- spelling checkers
- proof-reading

Spelling checkers

A spelling checker is an excellent tool, but, as the lager advert says: "It's good, but it's not that good."

What can spelling checkers do?

Spelling checkers compare the 'words' in your document with words held in a dictionary. Different dictionaries are available for different languages, such as English and American, so it is important that the correct dictionary is used.

An American spelling checker will reject 'colour' and 'fulfil' – in America, these words are spelt 'color' and 'fulfill'.

The spelling checker scans the text in your document, looking for spaces and full stops. These tell the spelling checker that a 'word' has just finished. The group of characters identified as a 'word' are then matched against the words in the dictionary.

If there is no match, it could mean one of two things:

1. You miskeyed the word, and it needs to be edited.
2. The dictionary does not have that word in its list, and – if the word is correct – it must be added to the dictionary.

What will spelling checkers miss?

If there is a match, it does not guarantee that you did not make a keying error! For example, if you press M instead of N (they are close on the keyboard) you could key in:

worm *instead of* worn

mane *instead of* name

The spelling checker will not catch 'worm' and 'mane' because they are correctly spelt words. So, you must use another check to be sure your finished work is perfect: proof-reading.

Proof-reading

A proof-read is a visual check of both the content and layout of material, including the positioning on the page of any figures and tables. There are two types of proof-reading:

1. comparing one draft against the next
2. reading through a draft

Both methods should be used.

Suppose you had a first draft, preferably double spaced, and you had written corrections all over it. Then you (or a friend) edited the text to correct it. Figure 4.25 shows an example of both documents.

First draft

The tag is punched with holes — to record the item type and other information —

Kimball tags are small pieces of card ~~punched with holes,~~ which can be attached to a garment,

is

and/torn off when the item is sold. *The part torn off is then input into a computer system*

Some stores use tags with bar codes nowadays. *This makes the process more automatic.*

More expensive items have a security tag which sets of an alarm if you try to leave the shop

without paying/ *for the goods*

Second draft

Kimball tags are small pieces of card which can be attached to a garment. The tag is punched
with holes – to record the item type and other information – and is torn off when the item is sold.
The part torn off is then input into a computer system.
Some stores use tags with bar codes nowadays. This makes the process more automatic.
More expensive items have a security tag which sets of an alarm if you try to leave the shop
without paying for the goods.

Figure 4.25 **Drafts of a document**

Your first job would be to proof-read the newer draft against the first
draft to make sure that all the planned corrections had been
implemented. You should check each correction, one at a time, and
tick them off as you go. You can then mark the second draft with any
corrections which were missed and still need to be done.

Then – and most importantly – you should file the old version away.
You may need to keep it for your portfolio folder (or you may file it in
the waste paper bin!).

Next – you must read the latest version through again. Does it still make
sense? Can you improve on it? Can you spot any mistakes that the spelling
checker missed? (There is one deliberate mistake. Can you find it?)

ACTIVITY 4.16

You need a partner for this activity.

1. Each of you key in three paragraphs. Do not look at the screen while
   you touch the keys, and work as fast as you can. This way you are
   likely to make quite a few mistakes! Save your file and print out two
   copies of your document.

2. Swap documents with your partner and spend five minutes proof-reading their work to find any errors.
3. Load your partner's document, make the corrections and resave your partner's file.
4. Print out the second draft and return both drafts to your partner.
5. Check the editing work your partner has done to your document, and mark any corrections that were missed.
6. Read through your own document once more, to see if you can spot any more errors.

Filenames

When you create a document you must think up a name for it for storage purposes. Then, next time you need the document, you can find the file by name.

There are restrictions on the names that you can use – and it is advisable to think carefully before choosing a name.

Limits on the number of characters

The filename is often limited in length, usually to 8 characters. Also some keyboard characters are not allowed, such as ':' and '.'.

ACTIVITY 4.17

Check your word processing package. What restrictions are there, if any, on the filenames you can use?

Choosing meaningful filenames

Choosing filenames is not a bit like choosing passwords! Passwords have to be kept secret so you try to think of a word which you can remember, which is special to you *and* that no one else might guess. Filenames are not secret, but *you* must be able to remember what you called your document, otherwise you might never find it again!

Choose names that make sense. Meaningful filenames which make the file contents obvious are best.

ACTIVITY 4.18

Guess which ONE of the following files contains details of the staff party plans:

a PENSION
b XMASDO
c MEMOTEN
d INVOICE

The evidence indicators

To prove you have covered the material of this element you need to produce at least two documents. Both documents must combine at least two sources of data (i.e. text, tables or graphics). Both must also include data taken from existing sources as well as data developed during input.

Your teacher/tutor will set you a task, e.g. to produce a business letter, a memo or a short report. You might also use a report written for another element as evidence for this unit.

5 Process graphic images

Introduction

This chapter covers the material needed for Element 2.2: Process graphic images.

The performance criteria state that the student must:

1. Identify **components of a graphic image**.
2. Select **image and page attributes** to create graphic images.
3. Create and **edit** graphic images.
4. Save and produce regular back-up copies.
5. Output graphic images.

The knowledge range

To meet the performance criteria, you *must* cover the range. The words shown in bold in the performance criteria above highlight the skills and knowledge you will need, and so we will now consider each of these in turn.

Note, first, that performance criteria 4 refers to back-up copies. This term has been met in Element 1.3 (page 86). Back-up copies of electronic files are made so that data can be recovered in the event of loss. These copies are normally kept in another building to avoid loss by fire or theft.

Note also that the most important part of this element is your practical use of a graphics software package. The activities in this chapter will lead you through the various ranged items and all the material you produce will be useful for your portfolio.

Components of a graphic image

Graphic images are drawings or artwork. They include:

- freehand drawn lines or curves
- geometric objects such as squares, rectangles and circles
- text messages
- areas of fill

Graphic images are commonly used in company logos or simple sketches. They might involve bitmap or vector graphic images drawn using a graphics software package, or could be bitmaps of photographs produced by a scanner.

There are many terms in the range statements which you will need to know (they are shown in bold):

- **Colour** – this includes shades of grey on printers that do not offer colour printing.
- **Lines** – lines have **width** and **style**.
- **Rectangles** – rectangles have **fill type**, **line type**, **line width**; they can have **square corners** or **rounded corners**.
- **Circles** – these can also have **fill type**, **line width** and **line style**.
- **Text** – this can be presented in a certain **style** and at a certain **size**, together these attributes define the **font**; use of fonts was covered in Chapter 4 (see page 109).
- When drawing, you can create special effects using **brush** or **spray** facilities.

Line width and style

The line **width** is the thickness of the line. Line thickness is different from line **style**. The line style can be dotted, double and so on. (See Figure 5.1.)

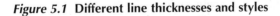

Figure 5.1 **Different line thicknesses and styles**

ACTIVITY 5.1

Find out what different line widths and line styles are available on your graphics software package.

Rectangles

Rectangles are drawn with lines: four lines joined at four right-angled corners. Each line can have its own line width and line style, but it would be more usual for all four to have the same width and style. We can then describe the line width and style of the whole rectangle.

Additional styles may also be used, e.g. a 'shadow' effect on two sides of the rectangle.

How you draw the rectangle depends on your graphics software package. Probably, you select 'rectangle', select where one corner will be and then drag the cursor, using the mouse, to the diagonally opposite corner, until the rectangle is as large as you want.

ACTIVITY 5.2

Find out how to draw a rectangle and what different widths and styles are available for drawing rectangles on your graphics software package.

Rectangles usually have square corners (that is how you see them in a maths class!). In graphics software packages, though, a 'friendlier' rectangle is often used – one with rounded corners (Figure 5.2).

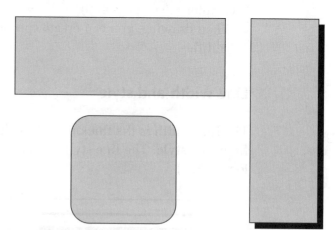

Figure 5.2 **Rectangle styles**

ACTIVITY 5.3

Find out what different styles of corners are available for drawing rectangles on your graphics software package.

A rectangle may be left empty, or it may be used to enclose a text message, or you may want to **fill** it with a colour or a pattern.

Fill options offered by graphics software packages vary, but usually there is a **palette** of colours and another of patterns to choose from. When you select a fill option, the area where your cursor currently points to changes – and the effect spreads outwards to the nearest boundary line. It is important that a shape you want to fill is 'closed', i.e. that there are no gaps in the lines forming the shape. Otherwise choosing fill results in your whole screen changing to the colour or pattern chosen!

ACTIVITY 5.4

Find out what different fill options are available on your graphics software package. Produce an A4 poster including at least three lines and eight different rectangles using different line widths, line styles, fill options and types of corners to show your findings from this and the previous three activities.

Circles

Circles, like rectangles, can be drawn with different line widths and line styles. You can also fill them in the same way.

Drawing the circle will not involve using a compass and the end effect will probably be much better than you might be able to do freehand. How you produce a circle depends on the graphics software package you are using. Probably, you first select 'circle' and decide where one point on the circumference, or where the centre, will be, and then you drag the cursor, using the mouse, until the circle is large enough (Figure 5.3).

Figure 5.3 **Circle styles**

ACTIVITY 5.5

Find out how to draw a circle and what different widths and styles are available for drawing circles on your graphics software package. Produce an A4 poster including at least eight different circles using different line widths, line styles and fill options to show your findings.

Brush and spray

If you were *not* using an IT system, what tools would you use? When you draw you usually use a pen or pencil to make lines and form shapes. When painting you may use a brush or a roller; this gives a different effect. If painting a large area, you might use a spray paint.

On an IT system, a graphics software package usually offers the same three tools: pencil, brush and spray. Each one produces a different effect. You can also vary the width of your pencil, or your brush. You can then be quite precise if you want to, or create broad strokes if that is the effect you want.

The brush and spray options are linked to the colour and pattern palettes so that you can 'spray' a colour or pattern onto the screen.

ACTIVITY 5.6

Find out how to use the brush and spray options on your graphics software package. Produce an A4 poster to show the variety of options available.

Image attributes

The term 'image attributes' means the things which describe the graphic image. This includes its height, width and the colours used.

The **height** of a graphic image is the distance from the top to the bottom. It can be measured in centimetres, inches or in lines of the page. You might specify 'full page' or 'half page' as the height, or be more precise and say '5 cm'.

The **width** of a graphic image is the distance from the left-hand side to the right-hand side. It will usually be measured in centimetres or inches (see Figure 5.4).

Figure 5.4 **Image attributes – height and width**

The maximum height of a graphic image is fixed first by the length of the page you are printing it on. The maximum width of a graphic image is also limited by the page size. At most, it could be the width of the page (although you would normally avoid using the margins). However, you normally want to keep the dimensions of a graphic image in proportion, so the height tends to be decided first, and then the width follows automatically.

How you control the size of a graphic image depends on your graphics software package. You may be able to specify exact measurements. You may be able to enlarge or reduce it to fit a frame within a page layout.

ACTIVITY 5.7

Find out how to control the size of a graphic image. Write notes so that someone new to your graphics software package would know what to do.

What **colours** you use will depend on your printing facilities. If you have no colour printer then you can only use shades of grey; these can be effective but not as effective as a splash of colour. You can use coloured paper – for black and white printing or for colour printing.

How many colours you can use will also be affected by your printing facilities; you may be limited to a few colours, or have a full palette of shades to choose from.

ACTIVITY 5.8

Find out what facilities you have for printing coloured graphic images. Find out how to print in colour rather than black and white. Find out how to use more than one colour at a time. Write notes so that someone new to your graphics software package would know what to do. Produce an A4 poster showing what facilities you have, and your ability to produce graphic images in colour.

Page attributes

In the same way as a graphic image has attributes such as height, width and colour, a page has attributes. These are: paper size, orientation and margins.

Paper size

Stationers use a coding system – A0, A1, A2, A3, A4, A5, etc. – to label different sizes of paper (Figure 5.5).

Most office IT systems have printers which accept A4 or smaller sized paper. For larger documents (e.g. plans) special plotters are needed.

ACTIVITY 5.9

Collect at least four different sized documents (A3 or smaller). Write a paragraph on each explaining its use and why its size was chosen. Store this work in your portfolio folder.

Orientation

Orientation is the direction of the print on a page (Figure 5.6):

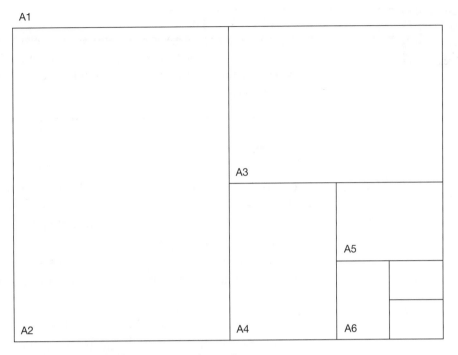

Figure 5.5 **How different paper sizes relate**

Portrait

Landscape

Figure 5.6 **Paper orientation**

- **Portrait** orientation prints across the width of the paper.
- **Landscape** orientation prints across the length of the paper.

The paper is fed into the printer in the normal way for both; with landscape orientation, the printing appears 'sideways'.

ACTIVITY 5.10

Collect two examples of both portrait and landscape orientation. Write notes explaining why each orientation has been used. Store this work in your portfolio folder.

Margins

Each page, whatever its size, would look strange if you printed right up to the edges. This would cause problems if you wanted to file the information. The hole punch may cut out something important; if you were to bind or staple pages together, it might be difficult to read all the information. With graphic images, it seems even more important to have a space around the artwork – so that the graphic image stands out.

There are four margins on each page: top, bottom, left and right. Any graphic images placed on a page would normally keep within the margins, that is, be placed within the main body of the page.

Margins were also discussed in Chapter 4 (see page 104).

Edit

You need to demonstrate that you can create and edit graphic images. By edit, we mean any of the following:

- cut
- copy
- move
- paste
- delete
- insert

Most of these terms are also used in other IT activities, e.g. word processing, spreadsheets and databases.

Notice though that cut and delete are not the same. To **cut** involves changing a graphic image to remove part of it. To **delete** involves removing the whole graphic image.

Copy and move have the same meanings as in document processing. You use **copy** to repeat a graphic image or part of it; you use **move** to change the position of a graphic image or part of it.

Paste allows you to bring in graphic images that were cut (or copied) from elsewhere, possibly from a library of clip-art or from some other graphic image you have drawn.

ACTIVITY 5.11

Design an A4 poster. Write down your graphic image attributes, and the page attributes that you plan to use. Using a graphics software package of your choice, first prepare a draft version of the poster, and on it handwrite what changes are needed to produce the final version. These two posters can be used to demonstrate that you can create and edit graphic images.

The evidence indicators

To prove you have covered the material of this element, you need to present two graphic images produced by yourself.

Records are also needed to show that you have:

- identified components of a graphic image
- selected image and page attributes
- created and edited graphic images
- saved your work regularly

6 Process numerical information

This chapter covers the material needed for Element 2.3: Process numerical information.

The performance criteria state that the student must:

1. Identify the **components** and **types of data** in a numerical processing problem.
2. Identify the **calculations** required to solve the problem.
3. Create a **layout** to enable numerical processing.
4. Enter, edit and delete data and add **titles** to the layout.
5. Use calculations to process numerical data.
6. Check for accuracy, save work regularly and output.

The knowledge range

To meet the performance criteria, you *must* cover the range. The words shown in bold in the performance criteria above highlight the skills and knowledge you will need, and so we now consider each of these in turn.

First, though, what is a numerical processing problem? It is a problem which involves calculations and/or formulae, such as:

- cost of goods sold in a small shop
- quantity of goods sold in a given time
- costs of electricity

This information enables calculations such as determining the profit, the number of goods remaining unsold and the total cost of overheads.

Often, these problems are solved using a spreadsheet software package (see Chapter 2). If you have never used a spreadsheet software package, now is the time to do so!

ACTIVITY 6.1

Draw a sketch of a spreadsheet, and label the rows and columns. Label a cell – the place where a row and column intersects. What kinds of data can you store in each cell of a spreadsheet?

Exactly how you use the spreadsheet software package depends on the package being used, and whether you are using a DOS-based or Windows-based system. A DOS-based system will use the keyboard only, using arrow keys to move about the spreadsheet and to highlight areas of the spreadsheet. A Windows-based system will use a mouse.

ACTIVITY 6.2

Find out how to load your spreadsheet software package. Find out how to enter the different types of data into a cell. Write notes on how to do this.

Components of a numerical processing problem

The components of a numerical processing problem include:

- items
- dates
- totals
- calculations

Items are the things about which calculations are necessary, e.g. goods, holidays, room bookings, number of people, quantity, costs, students and exam results.

Dates are important in most numerical processing problems. It is necessary to keep a record of when things are sold, when a holiday is booked and when the holiday is to start, when exams take place and when results will be available.

Totals are often needed: the total sales for a week, the total number of people booked for a holiday flight, the total number of items ordered, the total number of students entered for an examination and so on.

Calculations are also often needed. In invoicing, VAT (value added tax) at $17\frac{1}{2}$% has to be calculated. In payroll, PAYE (pay as you earn) tax and National Insurance (NI) contributions have to be calculated. In sales, a discount may be allowed, and a salesperson may earn a commission based on the number of sales made.

Numerical processing problems are often solved using a spreadsheet software package. The components of the numerical processing problem have to be placed within the spreadsheet structure to model the problem and find a solution.

Types of data

A spreadsheet can hold four different types of data:

- **numeric** – for numbers
- **dates** – in various formats, e.g. including the day of the week, excluding the year and so on
- **character** – for messages, text, labels and so on
- **formulae** – calculations based on other data within the spreadsheet

ACTIVITY 6.3

Compare this list of data types with those you wrote for Activity 6.1. Make sure you know how to enter each of these different data types. Check the notes produced in Activity 6.2, and update them if necessary.

It helps to identify the different components of a numerical processing problem and match their data types to those available on a spreadsheet software package.

The **item**, i.e. the thing we are interested in, will have a name or a description which can be stored as a string of characters. Examples could be holiday destinations such as SPAIN, PORTUGAL or FRANCE. It could be examinations such as GNVQ IT, GNVQ LEISURE AND TOURISM and GNVQ SCIENCE. These items will usually be placed as row or column titles in a text field.

Numeric data relating to the items will be stored as numeric data items. This will be all the numbers involved in the problem, e.g. the number of students entered for GNVQ IT, the number entered for GNVQ LEISURE AND TOURISM and so on. It is important that this data is entered with 100% accuracy. All calculations will be based on this data and so, if anything is incorrect, the results will be incorrect too.

Dates may be used to label rows or columns, or be part of the data used in a calculation. This may happen, for example, if the fine on a library book depends on the numbers of days it is overdue.

Formulae are used to make the calculations required to solve a problem. This could be a simple **total**, e.g. the cost of a list of items (calculated using a column sum), or a more complicated **calculation**, e.g. the cost of a quantity of goods (calculated as quantity times price) or the VAT due on an item (calculated as 0.175 times the price).

Calculations

Calculations are done automatically by the spreadsheet software package, so writing the formulae to perform the calculations is an important part of solving the numerical processing problem. All calculations that can be done on a calculator can also be done on spreadsheet software packages. This includes the usual four operations:

- addition
- subtraction
- multiplication
- division

ACTIVITY 6.4

Find out how to add two data items using a spreadsheet software package available to you. Find out how to subtract one data item from another. What symbols do you use for multiplication and division? How do you refer to data items in a cell of a spreadsheet within your formula? How do you get the result to appear in a particular cell?

One special formula allows you to **sum** a row or column of numerical data items. You must tell the software where to start adding, where to stop and where to put the result. Exactly how this is done will depend on your software package.

ACTIVITY 6.5

Find out how to add up all the numeric data items in a single row of a spreadsheet. Write down notes to explain this process to someone who does not know how to use your spreadsheet software package. Find out how to sum all the numeric data items in a column, rather than a row.

Layout of a spreadsheet

The spreadsheet is divided into **rows** and **columns** (Figure 6.1), although you would also include a **title** at the very top, and possibly a message at the bottom.

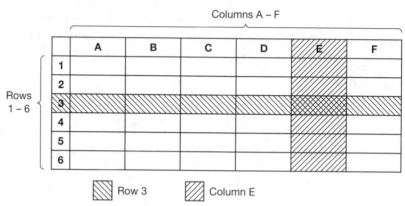

Figure 6.1 **Spreadsheet layout**

When designing a spreadsheet you decide how many rows and columns you will need. To begin with, all columns will have the same width – called the **default width** – which will be set by your spreadsheet software package.

ACTIVITY 6.6

Find out what the default width of columns is on your spreadsheet software package. What happens if you enter data that is wider than the column width? Does it matter what type of data you have entered? Are all data types treated in the same way?

If the **column width** is not wide enough to display your data, you will have to increase the width. You may also want to reduce the width of some columns, either to save paper or to improve the overall look of the spreadsheet.

ACTIVITY 6.7

Find out how to change the width of columns using your spreadsheet software package. Write notes on this which would help someone who has never used your spreadsheet software package before.

Sometimes, what you see on the screen does not match what is printed out. With some spreadsheet software packages, you think all your data can be seen, i.e. your column width is wide enough on the screen, but when you take a printout, some data is lost or **truncated**. This is a fault of the software, but it is up to you, the user, to check this carefully.

ACTIVITY 6.8

Experiment with different column widths – say 6, 7, 8, 9 and 10 units wide – and fill these columns with data of varying lengths. See if the data displayed is always printed in full.

Cell formats

If the data in each cell was presented just as you keyed it in, the end result would be quite unattractive and possibly difficult to read. Cell formats control the presentation of information in a cell. This is used to improve the overall look of the spreadsheet, and should make it easier for a reader to understand. For example, you can:

- control the position of text or labels, e.g. align text on its right-hand side to match numeric data in a column, or centre headings
- display numbers in currency format, e.g. with a pound sign preceding them
- decide on the number of decimal places to be shown, e.g. most currency is shown with two decimal places
- choose between different date formats, e.g. 'dd-mm-yy' or 'ddd-mmm-yyyy', or show time in the 24-hour format

ACTIVITY 6.9

Find out what display formats are offered with your spreadsheet software package. Enter some data into a spreadsheet and choose a variety of display options to show what you can do. Print out your spreadsheet, and make notes on how you achieved the effects shown.

Justification

It is important that information 'lines up' within the columns of a spreadsheet. This is called **justification** or **alignment**.

For text data, left alignment is normal for row titles and most data items. You might choose to centre the text (and its column heading) if you prefer.

For numeric data, which involves only whole numbers (integers), it is usual to use right alignment. Then the units are all in a line, and the tens are all in a line and so on. If the numbers have a decimal point (e.g. with a column of currency data) it would be normal to align on the decimal point. (See Figure 6.2.)

ACTIVITY 6.10

Find out how to control the alignment of a single cell of the spreadsheet. Find out how to control the alignment of a block of cells. Write notes on how to do this.

All text cells left aligned and all numeric cells right aligned

	A	B	C	D	E	F
1		Jan	Feb	Mar	April	TOTAL
2	Black	42	56	71	30	199
3	Blue	45	60	80	28	213
4	Green	12	15	20	9	56
5	Yellow	24	32	38	21	115
6		123	163	209	88	583

All data cells centred

	A	B	C	D	E	F
1		Jan	Feb	Mar	April	TOTAL
2	Black	42	56	71	30	199
3	Blue	45	60	80	28	213
4	Green	12	15	20	9	56
5	Yellow	24	32	38	21	115
6		123	163	209	88	583

Figure 6.2 **Different alignment within a spreadsheet**

Titles

It is important to include titles on your spreadsheet. Otherwise it may not be clear what the spreadsheet does, or when it was produced. There are several types of title within a spreadsheet:

- The **main title** appears at the very top and should include a description of the spreadsheet.
- At the top of each column you should have a **column title**, to label the data in that column.
- At the start of every row you should have a **row title**, to label the data in that row.

Some rows may be left blank for spacing purposes; these do not need row titles. Some rows may have lines of dashes to create the effect of a horizontal rule above a total; these do not need titles either.

Numeric data right aligned on a decimal tab

	A	B	C	D	E	F
1		Jan	Feb	Mar	April	TOTAL
2	Black	42	56	71	30	199
3	Blue	45	60	80	28	213
4	Green	12	15	20	9	56
5	Yellow	24	32	38	21	115
6		123	163	209	88	583

Showing decimal places

	A	B	C	D	E	F
1		Jan	Feb	Mar	April	TOTAL
2	Black	42.00	56.00	71.00	30.00	199.00
3	Blue	45.00	60.00	80.00	28.00	213.00
4	Green	12.00	15.00	20.00	9.00	56.00
5	Yellow	24.00	32.00	38.00	21.00	115.00
6		123.00	163.00	209.00	88.00	583.00

Figure 6.2 (continued)

Any row (or column) that has a **total** calculated from other rows (or columns) should be carefully labelled. (See Figure 6.3.)

Main title   Column titles

	A	B	C	D	E	F
1		Sales of A4 folders by month and colour				
2		Jan	Feb	Mar	April	TOTAL
3	Black	42.00	56.00	71.00	30.00	199.00
4	Blue	45.00	60.00	80.00	28.00	213.00
5	Green	12.00	15.00	20.00	9.00	56.00
6	Yellow	24.00	32.00	38.00	21.00	115.00
7	TOTAL	123.00	163.00	209.00	88.00	583.00

Row titles   Total titles

Figure 6.3 **Titles on a spreadsheet**

ACTIVITY 6.11

Create a spreadsheet with at least ten rows and at least five columns to solve a numerical processing problem. Enter data of all four types (text, numeric, totals and calculations). Adjust column widths to suit the data, and choose appropriate display options. Include a main title, column headings and row headings. Print out your spreadsheet, before and after editing it. Write notes on how you solved the numerical processing problem, and the calculations used in the spreadsheet.

The evidence indicators

To prove you have covered the material of this element you need to produce computer output showing that you have:

- created a layout to enable numerical processing
- entered, edited and deleted data and added titles to the layout
- used calculations to process numerical data
- checked your work for accuracy and saved it regularly

Records are also needed to show that you have:

- identified the components and types of data in a numerical processing problem
- identified the calculations required to solve the problem

7 Process structured data

Introduction

This chapter covers the material needed for Element 2.4: Process structured data.

The performance criteria state that the student must:

1. Identify the **database components** and **data types** in a given data handling problem.
2. Create a database to suit the problem.
3. Enter, edit and delete data.
4. Check data for **accuracy**.
5. Save work regularly and use **facilities** to generate reports.

The knowledge range

To meet the performance criteria, you *must* cover the range. The words shown in bold in the performance criteria above highlight the skills and knowledge you will need, and so we will now consider each of these in turn.

First, though, what is 'a given data handling problem'? It could be about people or about things. For example, names of people and their job titles and telephone numbers; destination of holidays booked; stock lists of goods such as software and the producer's name; cost of furniture and the costs of each item.

Database components

You have to be able to identify the database components in a given data handling problem. The two main components of databases are: records and fields. (See Figure 3.19, page 90.)

Records

The database file is divided into many **records**, all the same 'shape'; each record holds the same kind of information but about a different person or thing or event.

- If a database file keeps information about the employees in a company, for each employee there will be one record. The same information will be kept about each employee.
- If a database file keeps information about the products available for sale in a supermarket, one record will contain the details for a particular stock item. The same information will be kept about each stock item.
- If a database file keeps information about holiday bookings, one record will hold the information about one holiday booked. The same information will be kept about each booking.

ACTIVITY 7.1

Think of three different database files – related to people, things and events – and for each one write down what information may be kept in one record within that file.

Fields

In each record of the database file, there are a number of **fields**; these contain the data items.

- In the employee database file, the employee records will have fields for the employee's name, address, telephone number, job title, etc. (Figure 7.1(a)).
- In the product database file, the product records will have fields for product number, product description, price, quantity in stock, etc. (Figure 7.1(b)).
- In the holidays bookings database file, the bookings record will have fields for departure date, destination country, resort, date booked, customer details, etc. (Figure 7.1(c)).

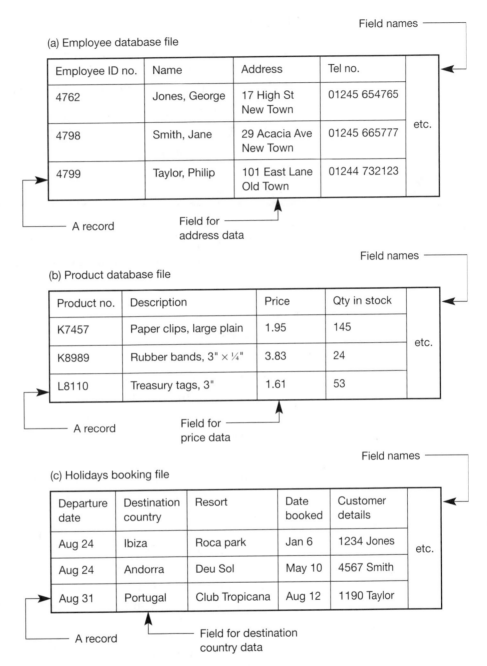

Field names

(a) Employee database file

Employee ID no.	Name	Address	Tel no.	
4762	Jones, George	17 High St New Town	01245 654765	etc.
4798	Smith, Jane	29 Acacia Ave New Town	01245 665777	
4799	Taylor, Philip	101 East Lane Old Town	01244 732123	

A record

Field for address data

Field names

(b) Product database file

Product no.	Description	Price	Qty in stock	
K7457	Paper clips, large plain	1.95	145	etc.
K8989	Rubber bands, 3" × ¼"	3.83	24	
L8110	Treasury tags, 3"	1.61	53	

A record

Field for price data

Field names

(c) Holidays booking file

Departure date	Destination country	Resort	Date booked	Customer details	
Aug 24	Ibiza	Roca park	Jan 6	1234 Jones	etc.
Aug 24	Andorra	Deu Sol	May 10	4567 Smith	
Aug 31	Portugal	Club Tropicana	Aug 12	1190 Taylor	

A record

Field for destination country data

Figure 7.1 **Different types of database files**

ACTIVITY 7.2

For your three different database files from Activity 7.1, write down what fields there will be in each record within the file.

Field names

When designing a database file, you need to list all the fields that will appear in each record. For each field, you need a unique field name. This field name will be used when you interrogate the database file.

For the employee database file the field names might be: EMP_NAME, EMP_ADDR, EMP_TELNO, EMP_JOBTITLE. It makes sense to choose field titles which are as meaningful as possible.

ACTIVITY 7.3

For one of the database files from Activity 7.1 (using your ideas from Activity 7.2) list the fields, using a unique name for each field.

Field lengths

Each field will have a data type: character, numeric, etc., and you will need to decide how much data needs to fit in, and therefore how long each field needs to be.

- When deciding on the length of text fields, look at some sample data and see what the longest possible entry could be. Choose a field length at least as long, perhaps a few characters more.
- When deciding on numeric fields, you are choosing not how it is stored (which is controlled by the software package) but how it is displayed:
  - How many decimal places will you need to produce the required level of accuracy? For money amounts, you usually use two places of decimals (for the pence), but on a telephone bill, for instance, you will notice more decimal places on the itemised list of call charges.
  - Do you want the pound sign to appear?
  - Do you want a comma to separate the figures in large amounts? For example, would you prefer to see '123,456' or '123456'?

- For dates, you also control how they are displayed rather than how the data is stored. Dates are actually stored as the number of days since some date a long time ago. Exactly when that starting date was will have been set up by someone when your software package was first installed.

ACTIVITY 7.4

Find out what date formats are available on your database software package. Write notes about this.

Data types

As mentioned before, there are three main data types that you need to know about:

- character
- number
- date

In the records of a product database file, there are fields for product number, product description, price, quantity in stock, etc. In deciding what data types to use to store or display this data, you need to think about the values it might have. The table below is an example.

Field	Possible values
Product number	Character string – only letters of the alphabet or numbers, no decimal point or other characters
Product description	Text (character string) – may include numbers, for example to describe dimensions of product
Price	Currency – two decimal places for pence
Quantity in stock	Number – integer, cannot be less than zero

ACTIVITY 7.5

These are the fields in the database for holiday bookings: departure date, destination country, resort, date booked, customer details. For each field, suggest what values the data might take, and create a table (as above) to record this information.

Accuracy

It is important that the data in a database be accurate, because it is quite likely that decisions will be made based on reports produced from the data. Reliable, accurate and up-to-date information is essential. How can this be achieved? Where do inaccuracies happen? If you follow the flow of information, you will see that there are many places where errors can happen, and inaccurate data can result.

First, where does the data come from? Usually, it is captured on a document (called a **source document**). Here are some examples of source documents:

- an order form completed by a salesperson
- a cheque written to pay a bill
- a gas meter reading
- a clock card showing at what times a person was at work during a week
- an application form for a loan

Some of the information will be handwritten, so it is important that it is legible. (Remember this next time you are filling in a form!) Some of the information might have to be read automatically by a machine. Examples include the magnetic ink writing on the bottom of a cheque. (See Chapter 3, page 82, for more information about **data capture**.)

One point at which errors creep in is when the data is entered into the IT system. To try to prevent this we use **validation** techniques to catch any data which may be incorrect.

Validity

For each field, you can decide what data values would be valid – i.e. acceptable and/or reasonable to expect. More importantly, you decide the values which would be invalid. For example:

- the date 32/2/99 is invalid
- the time 31.04 is invalid
- the age 22 is invalid if entry to a youth club is limited to 10- to 16-year-olds

Here is the data table for the product database record.

Field	Valid data	Invalid data
Product number	Character string – only letters of the alphabet or numbers	Decimal point and any other punctuation characters
Product description	Text (character string) – may include numbers	None
Price	Currency – two decimal places for pence	No letters or punctuation characters (except decimal point)
Quantity in stock	Number – integer	Cannot be less than zero, no decimal point

ACTIVITY 7.6

Look again at the fields in the database for holiday bookings: departure date, destination country, resort, date booked, customer details. For each field, suggest what values would be valid, and what values you would say are invalid. Add this information to the table you created in Activity 7.5.

Having decided what values could be valid you can specify this in the database design. Then, when data is entered, only valid data will be accepted.

ACTIVITY 7.7

Find out how to specify valid data for each field in a database file. Write notes on this.

Correctness

Data may be valid but incorrect. An example might be the entry of first name as 'Pieter' which could be valid but is probably incorrect and should perhaps be 'Peter'. Unfortunately, there is no way for the software to check for this type of error. You have to rely on careful keying by the data entry clerk, and careful checking against the original document (called **verification**) to trap this type of error.

Facilities

Having set up a database of records, you will need to interrogate the data, to find things out. For this, you will need to use two different facilities that are part of every database software package: sort and search.

These two terms are easily confused, but it is important that you know which to use, and how you can produce the required reports from your database file.

Sort

The word 'sort' is used in many ways. If you look it up in the thesaurus of your word processor, you will find it is either a noun or a verb. For the noun, my word processor offers all these alternatives for the word sort:

bracket	family	lot	sector
breed	genre	mould	set
cast	genus	nature	species
category	group	order	style
class	grouping	persuasion	type
division	ilk	section	variety

For the verb, the thesaurus offers many more words! (Mine offers 55 words. If you have never used a thesaurus, now is the time. Key in the word 'sort' and position your cursor on the word while you select the thesaurus facility. See what happens.)

In IT, sorting used to mean rearranging records in a file into some order, typically numerical or alphabetical. The telephone directory is sorted in alphabetical order by surname. It is also sorted by a second field – the first name – so that 'Jones, John' comes before 'Jones, Peter'.

With most modern software, the records may be stored in any order, usually the order they were entered. The order in which they are printed out is controlled by key fields and index files which the software creates to keep track of the location of each record.

In IT, then, to sort a database means to present a listing of items in a given order.

ACTIVITY 7.8

Create a database file to hold ten records of information. Sort your records on one numeric field, and print out the data. Sort the data by one alphabetic field and print it out.

You might decide to use a spreadsheet package to store database information. This works well until you decide to sort the data. Because the rows and columns of a spreadsheet do not necessarily correspond to the records and fields of a database, some software packages allow you to sort the items in one column (say), leaving all the other data items where they are. If you do this the data belonging to one record will appear in the row of another record!

ACTIVITY 7.9

Create a spreadsheet to hold data for five records of information.
Investigate how sorting is done. See if you can sort one column at a time.

Search

Searching is different from sorting. To search a database the software looks through all the records in a database to locate a specific occurrence of a piece of text or a number. For example, a search for 'Edward' might find one occurrence for 'Edward Blake', while a search for 'Blake' might find two occurrences, one for 'Edward Blake' the other for 'Martin Blake'. The records are not sorted during a search – unless you tell the software to do so for any printout produced.

ACTIVITY 7.10

Access a database and search for a particular record of interest to you. (Refer to your notes from Activities 3.10, 3.11 and 3.12.)

The evidence indicators

To prove you have covered the material of this element you need to construct a simple database – a single database resulting in one main datafile. The file should have 20 records, with four or five fields per record.

Computer output will be needed to show that you have:

- identified the data components and data types in a given data handling problem
- entered, edited and deleted data
- checked data for accuracy
- saved your work regularly and used facilities to generate reports

Wordsearch 2

These words have been used in Unit 2, find them in the wordsearch below:

CALCULATION	EMBOLDEN	LAYOUT	SEARCH
CHARACTER	FIELD	LINE	SORT
CIRCLE	FILE	MARGIN	SPELLCHECK
COLOUR	FILENAME	NUMBER	SPRAY
COLUMN	FILL	ORIENTATION	TAB
COPY	FONT	PASTE	TABLE
CUT	FORMAT	PORTRAIT	TEXT
DATA	GRAPHIC	PROOFREAD	TOTAL
DATABASE	IMAGE	RECORD	UNDERLINE
DATE	JUSTIFICATION	RECTANGLE	
DELETE	LANDSCAPE	ROW	

E	G	F	O	R	I	E	N	T	A	T	I	O	N	D
L	R	I	R	E	M	B	O	L	D	E	N	M	M	A
B	A	L	E	C	A	A	I	A	E	X	C	N	U	T
A	P	E	T	T	R	T	T	E	L	T	O	S	L	A
T	H	N	C	A	G	E	A	O	E	I	P	C	O	B
K	I	A	A	N	I	G	L	D	T	L	Y	O	C	A
T	C	M	R	G	N	A	U	A	E	A	Y	L	O	S
I	U	E	A	L	U	M	C	E	N	N	L	O	P	E
A	T	L	H	E	N	I	L	R	E	D	N	U	Z	N
R	R	L	C	C	F	P	A	F	L	S	A	R	Y	H
T	E	I	A	I	L	I	C	O	I	C	O	A	C	F
R	B	F	T	Y	R	L	N	O	F	A	R	R	L	I
O	M	S	D	R	O	C	E	R	B	P	A	S	T	E
P	U	S	N	D	W	U	L	P	S	E	E	N	I	L
J	N	F	O	R	M	A	T	E	S	F	O	N	T	D

Sample test for Unit 2

Check that you have understood the material of this unit by doing these sample external test questions.

These questions have been based on questions set by two of the three awarding bodies for GNVQ: RSA and City & Guilds. The questions set by BTEC are similar.

Each question offers four options, but only one of them is correct. At the end of this book, the correct answers are given.

Read each question very carefully before making your decision.

Question 1 A letter or report which uses different styles of fonts has:

    a   lots of different pictures
    b   different print character styles
    c   many pages
    d   left and right margins

Question 2 A letter or report which has full justification has:

    a   every line centred
    b   a ragged right-hand margin
    c   straight left-hand and right-hand margins
    d   every line in capital letters

Question 3 A tab would be useful when:

    a   underlining a heading
    b   inputting a table of figures
    c   using a keyboard
    d   using a mouse

Question 4 Which ONE of the following must be used to edit the word 'create' into 'crate'?

    a   insert
    b   amend
    c   copy
    d   delete

Question 5 Which ONE of the following could be used to highlight an important word in a document?

a   embolden
b   copy
c   move
d   cut and paste

Question 6 Which ONE of the following keying errors will be spotted by a spelling checker?

a   this jumper is **worm** out
b   the dog **ram** away
c   **raim** stopped play
d   the **sum** is shining

Question 7 A document contains details of procedures for evacuating a building in case of fire. Which ONE of the following filenames would be most meaningful for this?

a   HOTEL7
b   LET1709
c   PROC6
d   FIRE95

Question 8 Figure T2.1 shows a shape with:

a   curved corners
b   crossed corners
c   rounded corners
d   squared corners

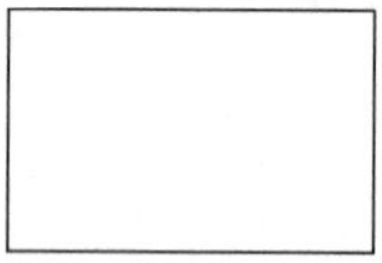

Figure T2.1

Question 9 Figure T2.2 shows a shape that has been:

a   inserted
b   filled
c   circled
d   deleted

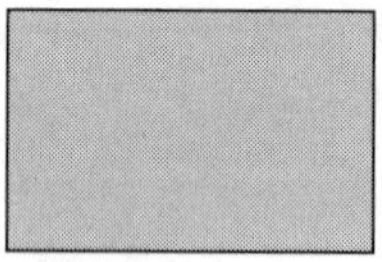

Figure T2.2

Question 10 To change image P to image Q in Figure T2.3 which ONE of the following would be used?

a   line style
b   line width
c   line colour
d   line circle

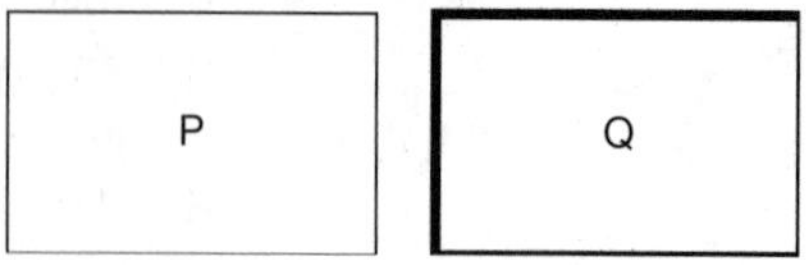

Figure T2.3

Question 11   In Figure T2.4, which ONE of the following would be used to change shape X to shape Y?

a   height
b   width
c   spacing
d   font

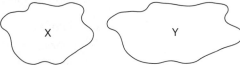

Figure T2.4

Question 12   Which ONE of the following describes the blank area surrounding a picture on a page?

a   tabs
b   margins
c   paragraphs
d   indents

Question 13   To change image J to image K in Figure T2.5 which ONE of the following functions has been used to add the extra window?

a   fill
b   move
c   delete
d   copy

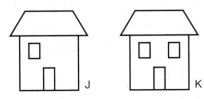

Figure T2.5

Question 14   In Figure T2.6, which ONE of the following functions would be used to change image L to image M to remove the windows?

a   insert
b   copy
c   delete
d   paste

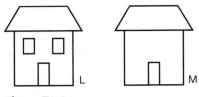

Figure T2.6

Question 15   Which ONE of the following could be used to calculate VAT in a column on a spreadsheet?

    a   date
    b   character
    c   digit
    d   formula

Question 16   Refer to Figure T2.7. To get the total price of black pens (column D) from the quantity and unit price of black pens (columns B and C) which ONE of the following would be used?

    a   subtraction
    b   multiplication
    c   fraction
    d   ratio

	A	B	C	D
1	STATIONERY SHOP			
2	ITEM	QUANTITY	UNIT PRICE	TOTAL PRICE
3	Black pens	1023	£0.45	£460.35
4	Red pens	405	£0.45	£182.25
5	Black pencils	680	£0.23	£156.40
6	Red pencils	293	£0.23	£67.39
7		2401		£866.39

Figure T2.7

Question 17   Refer to Figure T2.7. Which ONE of the following could be used to total up column B (total quantity of pens and pencils = 2401)?

    a   subtraction
    b   division
    c   multiplication
    d   sum

Question 18   Refer to Figure T2.7. Which ONE of the following could be used to make sure all the words in column A started in the same place?

    a   justification
    b   emboldening
    c   underlining
    d   paragraphs

Question 19   Refer to Figure T2.8. Which ONE of the following is shown by the shaded area?

a   a character
b   a formula
c   a column
d   a row

SALES OF FRUIT				
Fruit	1991	1992	1993	TOTAL
Grapes	10	15	20	45
Oranges	5	8	10	23
Bananas	20	30	40	90
Total	35	53	70	158

Figure T2.8

Question 20   Refer to Figure T2.8. The entry SALES OF FRUIT is

a   a row title
b   a column title
c   a main title
d   a centred title

Question 21   Refer to Figure T2.8. The entries 1991, 1992 and 1993 are examples of:

a   row titles
b   column titles
c   main titles
d   centred titles

Question 22   Refer to Figure T2.9 (overpage). Which ONE of the following is shown shaded?

a   a field
b   a file
c   a record
d   a file length

Question 23   Refer to Figure T2.9. Which ONE of the following points to the field names?

a   P
b   Q
c   R
d   S

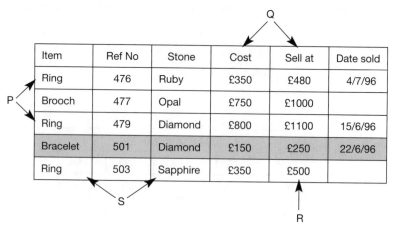

Figure T2.9

Question 24 Refer to Figure T2.10. Which ONE of the following is shown in column 3?

a field type
b record number
c field name
d field length

Column 1	Column 2	Column 3	Column 4
1	Item	character	10
2	Ref No	numeric	3
3	Stone	character	10
4	Cost	currency	6
5	Sell at	currency	6
6	Date sold	date	8

Figure T2.10

Question 25 Refer to Figure T2.10. Which ONE of the following is shown in column 4?

a field type
b record number
c field name
d field length

> **Text A**
> - only values that will be used for calculations
> - could include a decimal point
> - allows leading + or – signs

Question 26   Which ONE of the following obeys the rules given in Text A?

    a   character
    b   number
    c   date
    d   filename

Question 27   Data, including name and height, is being entered on a database. It is decided that, from the information in Text B, to use a validity range of 0.5–2.75 m for the height data. Which ONE of the following would be rejected by this validity test?

    a   Robert Jones, 1.62 m
    b   Amelia Payne, 3.53 m
    c   Roger Griffiths, 2.30 m
    d   Alice Monk, 1.93 m

> **Text B**
> According to the Guinness Book of records, the tallest recorded person was Robert Wadlow. He was 8 ft 11.2 inches tall – or 2.72 m. The shortest person was Pauline Musters at 1 ft 11.2 inches – 0.59 m.

Question 28   Which ONE of the following would an accuracy check identify as a valid date?

    a   01 Mep 94
    b   35/09/94
    c   01/09/94
    d   21/14/94

Question 29   Which ONE of the following results in a rearrangement of records in a given order?

    a   browse
    b   search
    c   sort
    d   view

Investigating working with information technology

This section covers the material needed for Unit 3: Investigating working with information technology.

There are three chapters which match the three elements in Unit 3:

- Chapter 8 covers Element 3.1: Examine working with information technology
- Chapter 9 covers Element 3.2: Explore jobs that involve working with information technology
- Chapter 10 covers Element 3.3: Plan for employment that involves working with information technology

These three chapters provide valuable information for everyone, even if you do not plan to look for a job straight away.

You may decide that a particular job suits you, but that you will need more training and better qualifications before you will be considered for such a post.

External test

For this unit, the external test has approximately 30 multiple choice questions. A complete test covering the whole unit is given at the end of Chapter 10; the answers to this test are given at the end of the book.

8 Examine working with information technology

This chapter covers the material needed for Element 3.1: Examine working with information technology.

The performance criteria state that the student must:

1. Identify and give examples of **jobs** which involve working with information technology.
2. Identify and give examples of **organisations** that employ people to do these jobs.
3. **Compare ways** in which organisations prepare, process and present information.

The knowledge range

To meet the performance criteria, you *must* cover the range. The words shown in bold in the performance criteria above highlight the skills and knowledge you will need and so we will now consider each of these in turn.

Jobs

To find out about jobs available which involve working with IT, you will need to study several sources:

- local newspapers
- national press
- computer press

ACTIVITY 8.1

Make a list of local and national newspapers and find out if they concentrate on vacancies in IT on a particular day of the week. Do they print an 'IT supplement'? Find out the names of publications in the computer press. Try to arrange to receive copies of these publications, or make regular visits to your local library to refer to them.

The jobs which involve working with IT fall into three main groups:

1. **users** – that's almost everyone nowadays
2. **service providers** – the help desk, service engineers, etc.
3. **IT producers** – the technical 'whizz kids' who design hardware and write software

ACTIVITY 8.2

Study recent advertisements to identify three examples of users of IT, three examples of service providers and three examples of IT producers. Cut out (or make a copy of) and keep the advertisements, noting the date and source of the publication.

Using IT

The list of people using IT is almost endless. In fact, it might be quicker to make a list of the people who do not use IT, since there are so few areas of business left that have not begun to use IT. IT, as you have already studied in earlier elements, is used for:

- processing documents
- processing numerical data
- producing graphics
- creating, maintaining and interrogating databases
- controlling production processes

ACTIVITY 8.3

From the advertisements of your three users of IT (from Activity 8.2) identify the type of work they are offering. Which software packages would the successful applicant need to be able to use?

Providing IT services

Many jobs have been lost though the introduction of computerised techniques, but at the same time new jobs have been created, many of them providing IT services such as:

- user support
- system maintenance
- hardware and software maintenance
- servicing and repair
- network management
- database management

ACTIVITY 8.4

From the advertisements of your three IT service providers (from Activity 8.2) identify the type of work they are offering. Which software packages would the successful applicant need to know about?

Providing IT products

The manufacture of the products themselves have also generated new job opportunities, for instance in:

- IT systems design
- software production
- manufacture
- publishing

ACTIVITY 8.5

From the advertisements of your three IT producers (from Activity 8.2) identify the type of work they are offering. What kind of work would the successful applicant be asked to do?

Organisations

The organisations involved in IT can be divided into two main groups:

1. those providing a product or service – the IT suppliers
2. those using the products or services – the IT users

IT users

The list is endless! Here are a few examples you have already studied:

- shops
- factories
- banks
- booking agencies
- offices

ACTIVITY 8.6

Write down four more examples of organisations who use IT. For each one, list three separate jobs within that organisation where IT would be used the most.

IT suppliers

IT suppliers include four main types:

- computer manufacturers
- software producers
- computer shops
- IT maintenance and support agencies

In some parts of the UK there is a greater opportunity to find work in organisations which supply IT products – not because unemployment is lower in these areas, but because these types of organisation seem to develop close to each other.

ACTIVITY 8.7

For each of the four types of IT suppliers listed above, find three examples of recent advertisements. What types of job vacancies do these organisations have? Where are the organisations located?

Comparison between organisations

In examining working with IT, it is important to notice how organisations prepare, process and present information. Any comparison needs to be on the basis of the following criteria:

- Speed – how quickly can the job be done?
- Ease of use – how much training is needed before you can use the system successfully?
- Effort – how many people are needed to complete the work?
- Accuracy – is it possible to achieve 100% accuracy?

ACTIVITY 8.8

In 1975, an office worker was employed to use an electric typewriter to produce letters reminding customers to pay overdue invoices. Twenty-five years later, another office worker uses a mailmerge facility to do the same job. Compare these two jobs using the four criteria listed above.

Ways of preparing, processing and presenting information

There are two main methods to consider: manual methods (i.e. without using a computer) and automatic methods (using a computer).

Manual methods can be efficient and effective in getting a particular job done. Indeed, most jobs now done by an IT system were done manually at one time. The processes involved are similar – the IT system just does some things faster, can handle larger volumes of data, cross-reference information more easily and communicate across vast distances using telecommunications with ease.

When working with IT, not all things will be done using IT. There may be some parts of a job that are still done manually.

- A manager of a small shop may use an IT system to prepare orders and to keep details of stock, but the payroll – especially if only two or three people are employed – will probably be done manually.
- The owner of a small company may have thousands of customers and send out hundreds of invoices each week, but have only 25 suppliers and receive at most 30 invoices each month. Because of the volumes involved in these two systems, the company may produce invoices weekly on an IT system but keep the purchase ledger accounts (the amounts owed to suppliers) on a manual system.

ACTIVITY 8.9

Identify an organisation which uses IT for some parts of their business, but not all. Why have they not computerised the manual processes?

Automated methods apply not only to the processing of information, but also to the methods used to prepare information for entry to an IT system. We have already looked at data capture methods in Chapter 3.

ACTIVITY 8.10

Mark sensing is used by banking IT systems to reading the MICR characters on the bottom of cheques. This ensures that the account and cheque details are correctly recorded when a cheque is presented for payment. Make a list of three other methods of mark sensing. Give two examples of the use of each method. Explain why automated methods are better for collecting the data than manual methods.

ACTIVITY 8.11

Choose two organisations and suggest tasks they may do using IT. Compare the methods they use to prepare, process and present information. (At least one of your organisations must use IT.)

The evidence indicators

To prove you have covered the material of this element you need to make a list:

- identifying different types of jobs, covering the range and providing two examples of each type of job
- identifying different organisations that employ people to do these jobs and providing two examples of each type of organisation

A summary is also needed comparing the ways that two different organisations prepare, process and present information.

9 Explore jobs that involve working with information technology

Introduction

This chapter covers the material needed for Element 3.2: Explore jobs that involve working with information technology.

The performance criteria state that the student must:

1. Identify **jobs** involving working with information technology that would **suit** her/him.
2. Describe **what is involved** in each job and explain why it would **suit** her/him.
3. Identify the main **skills** and **qualifications** required for each identified job.
4. Identify how s/he could obtain these **skills** and **qualifications**.
5. Seek **advice** and **information** from **appropriate sources** when necessary.

The knowledge range

To meet the performance criteria, you *must* cover the range. The words shown in bold in the performance criteria above highlight the skills and knowledge you will need and so we will now consider each of these in turn.

Jobs

Within the IT industry there are many different types of jobs. Here is a list of job titles:

- computer operator
- data processing manager
- data preparation clerk
- programmer
- systems programmer
- applications programmer
- information system engineers
- coders
- systems analyst
- systems designer
- technical support staff
- computer service engineer
- software support staff

One way of learning about the jobs available in an industry is to study the advertisements.

ACTIVITY 9.1

Find examples of advertisements for jobs for each of the job titles listed above. Use the same sources of advertisements you used in Chapter 8, and try to get a cross-section of the three types of job opportunities: using IT, providing IT services and providing IT products.

One way of finding out what jobs may suit you is to investigate what is involved in the job.

ACTIVITY 9.2

Read all the advertisements you have collected and try to decide what each job actually involves. Make notes for each job title and then compare them with the list below.

- A **computer operator** is the person who operates the IT system and, where appropriate, responds to requests from the operating system and from remote users in a time-sharing system.
- A **data processing manager** is the person responsible for the overall running of a data processing department.
- **Data preparation staff** are responsible for organising and entering data into the IT system.
- A **programmer** is the person responsible for writing and testing

computer programs. Those involved in the writing of operating systems, general utilities (such as sort routines) and specialist tools (such as a graphical user interface) are usually called **systems programmers**, while those writing programs for specific user applications are known as **applications programmers**.

Those programmers working on the design and testing of programs are often called **information systems engineers**, while those who are mostly involved in translating statements into machine readable form are called **coders.**

- The **systems analyst/systems designer** is responsible for the analysis of a system to assess its suitability for computerisation. Where computerisation is decided upon, the systems designer will be responsible for building on the analyst's results to create the new computer-based system and will normally continue to work up to the point where programmers can sensibly take over.

  Where a person who has been responsible for the analysis then works on the new system design, they are referred to as an **analyst/designer.**

- **Technical support staff** are IT specialists who are concerned with the integrity and functionality of the IT system. They may be hardware oriented rather than software oriented.

- The **computer service engineer** is the person responsible for the maintenance of the hardware, and is often employed by a specialist contract servicing company.

- **Software support staff** are usually employed by software houses or specialist vendors. They respond to questions relating to the use of particular pieces of software. Often, software support staff are referred to as a '**help desk**' and may be contacted quickly using the **telephone** '**hot line**' to give advice on problem solving.

All jobs within an industry will be in a 'pecking order'. Usually everyone starts at the bottom, and slowly – or quickly – works their way up the ladder of success. Having extra qualifications may mean you can jump a few rungs on the ladder, although you will have spent time gaining your qualifications. Someone with on-the-job experience, but fewer qualifications, may also make good progress. A lot depends on the type of job you are doing and how you approach your work.

One important measure of a job is the salary it offers. Some jobs offer a 'negotiable' salary. That means the prospective employer may measure you by what you've earned to date, rather than what the job on offer demands from you.

ACTIVITY 9.3

Classify the advertisements you collected in Activity 9.1 by salary offered. Note also the previous experience, or qualifications, required for each job.

Jobs suitable as initial employment

Not all the jobs advertised will suit you if you are looking for your first job. In fact, you may find that hardly any of them seem to suit you at all! This may be because you have been looking in the wrong place, i.e. the wrong newspapers. In the next chapter, we look at where you might seek vacancies straight after finishing your GNVQ course.

ACTIVITY 9.4

Make a note of any companies that were advertising for applicants with little or no experience. It would be helpful to write to them to ask about possible vacancies for when your course ends, about training opportunities they might offer and to find out exactly what qualifications they expect from applicants.

Jobs suitable for further progression in the sector

Certainly, most of the advertisements looked at so far will give you some ideas about how you can progress within the IT industry.

Some job titles include the words 'junior' or 'senior' to show that, with experience, there is an opportunity to advance to jobs with more responsibility (and more pay!).

Jobs that suit you

Most people spend two-thirds of their time awake; some need less sleep and have longer waking hours.

When you do start work, the time spent at work – and travelling to and from work – can take as much as 70% of your waking day. If you work a five-day week and count weekends as free time, this can become close to 50% of your total available time.

How the day goes by

It is very important to find a job that you like. Otherwise, half your life may be spent doing something you do not enjoy.

How can you decide what type of job will suit you? From a prospective employer's point of view, you might also consider what it is about you that might suit the job on offer.

There are three main things to consider:

- your own circumstances
- your interests
- the available opportunities

Matching your own circumstances

You could start with some self-evaluation, by making a list describing yourself. Be honest about your good points and your faults.

ACTIVITY 9.5

Write down eight things about yourself which you might be proud to tell a prospective employer. Write down four things which you might not want that employer to know.

Compare your list with the checklist below. Did you consider any of these points to be important?

- What age are you? Are you married? Do you have any children – or other dependants – to support?
- What qualifications do you have? Would you be willing to do more training to gain more qualifications?
- What work experience do you have? Do you have any references from previous employers?
- Where do you live? Do you live at home with your parents? Do you live in rented accommodation, or in your own home? Would you be willing to move to get a job?

- Do you have your own transport? Do you have a clean driver's licence? How would you get to and from work?
- How do you look? Are you careful about your appearance? Do you have clothes that would be good enough to wear to an interview? Do you have clothes that would be suitable to wear to work?
- How are you with people? Do you feel confident when meeting people for the first time? Are you good at remembering names of people you meet?
- Do you plan things? Are you organised – a natural list-writer? Are you always on time?

- Is your handwriting neat and legible? Are you good on the telephone? Can you leave a sensible message on an answering machine?
- How good are you working with IT?

Hopefully, this last question will be one that you can answer with a definite and positive answer. What about the others? Are there things you need to improve on, which will increase your chances of getting a job?

ACTIVITY 9.6

Look back at your list of eight good things and four not-so-good things from Activity 9.5. Can you add more good things to say about yourself? Are there things you will need to work on to make yourself more attractive to a prospective employer?

Your interests

You may think that the important deciding factor when selecting an applicant for a job is their qualifications. This is true, but when faced with several applicants, all with the same qualifications, how can an employer make a choice?

The impression you give at an interview will be important.

- Were you confident?
- Did you 'look the part'?
- Did you answer the questions in a friendly and yet respectful way?
- Did you have some useful questions to ask – not just about how long the lunch break was and how many days holiday you would get!

To be invited for interview, you will have had to impress the employer with your application form.

- Did you complete the form – answering all questions?
- Was your handwriting neat and legible? (Figure 9.1.)

Faced with ten application forms, all from people with the required qualifications, the employer can then only look at 'extracurricular' activities – what you do in your spare time.

Employers are more likely to be interested in you if you have outside interests that will help you to get on with other people who already work for the company.

- If you list your interests as 'watching TV' you will have this in common with millions of TV viewers, but it does suggest you spend your time being entertained, rather than meeting people and sharing some interest.
- At the other extreme, if you say your main interest is 'dancing at clubs', the prospective employer will wonder if your social life will interfere with normal working hours. Will you be fresh for work every Monday morning?

Most employers will be glad to see that you are involved in some sporting activity – doing it rather than watching – because this would suggest a healthier lifestyle.

ABC Co Ltd
High Road, Anytown

APPLICATION FORM - Junior clerk, IT department

Please complete this form in BLOCK CAPITALS. Thank you.

NAME:	*Jim Sharpe*
ADDRESS:	*14 Albert Drive* *Newtown, Hants* *RG14 3PQ*
POST CODE:	

Please list qualifications held including grades obtained.

DATE OF QUALIFICATION	LEVEL e.g. GCSE	SUBJECT	GRADE OBTAINED
June 96	GCSE	ENGLISH	B
''		MATHS	D
''		SCIENCE	DD
''		HISTORY	C
''		GEOGRAPHY	C
''		ENGLISH LIT	C
''		BUSINESS ST.	E
''		ART	E
''		DRAMA	D

Please give the names and addresses of <u>two</u> referees. One should be your last employer or headteacher.

1st referee

NAME:	MRS P RUDGE (head mistress)
ADDRESS:	C/O TRINITY HIGH SCHOOL SCHOOL LANE ANYTOWN
POST CODE:	GU14 9LU

2nd referee

NAME:	MR T PINK (employer)
ADDRESS:	THE KETCH FISH BAR ST MARKS HILL ROAD
POST CODE:	GU20 4TZ

Send your completed application form, together with a covering letter telling us more about yourself, to Miss S Jones, Personnel Manager, ABC Co Ltd, High Road, Anytown.

<u>Closing date for applications: 31st August 1996</u>

Figure 9.1 **Example of a bad job application**

ACTIVITY 9.7

Write a paragraph describing your interests. This will be useful when creating your CV.

ACTIVITY 9.8

Working with a partner, role play the first few minutes of an interview. Practise saying two or three sentences in reply to the question: 'Tell me something about yourself.' See how quickly you can interest the interviewer with facts about yourself.

What does the job involve?

Before you decide to apply for a job, you must check that you would be prepared to do whatever is involved.

- When would you be required to work? Does it involve shift working?
- Would you need to wear a special uniform or outfit?
- Would you need to do further training, say one day a week at college?
- Would you need to travel away from home?
- Where would you work? In a quiet office? In a busy, noisy office? With lots of other people? On your own? Indoors? Outdoors?

If the job involves some condition that would make you unhappy, then the long-term prospects for you doing that job would not be good. Instead, try to find work that suits you – or think about changing your approach to what you do or do not like doing.

ACTIVITY 9.9

What conditions would appeal to you? What conditions do you think you would not be willing to accept? Make a list, so you can use it later to decide whether to apply for a particular job.

Tasks of a job

Each day, most of your time will be spent 'doing the job'. What tasks will it involve?

- Will there be lots of paperwork? Will you be working at a workstation all day?

- How will your time be spent? On the telephone? Making calls? Receiving calls?
- Will you be doing the same thing all day, or will there be some variety in your work?

It is important that you realise the pressures that might build up if presented with working conditions that are too stressful for you. While you might not recognise it, your body soon starts to show symptoms of stress: headaches or migraines, falling prey to colds, back pains.

Be honest with yourself about what you enjoy doing and what irritates you. Aim to find the type of work that will let you perform well, not get you down.

ACTIVITY 9.10

What types of task appeal to you? What things do you not like doing? Make a list, so you can use it later to decide whether to apply for a particular job.

Responsibilities of a job

When you first start work, it is unlikely that you will be given responsibility for other people. However, you may be given responsibility for certain tasks in the office.

- It may be your job to answer the telephone and pass the call on to someone else or, if they are out, to take a message.
- It may be your job to welcome visitors, to take their coat and fetch them a cup of coffee.
- It may be your job to write up a list of all outgoing mail, to stick the stamps on the envelopes and take the mail to the local post office.
- It may be your job to file all correspondence, or send faxes, or do the photocopying for everyone else in the office.

When you first start, you may feel that these tasks – including making tea for the boss – means you are being used as a dogsbody. You may feel you can do more, but that you are not being given the opportunity to use your skills.

You need to be patient. These tasks may seem lowly, but the smooth running of an office involves many such tasks and to start with you will be given very easy things to do. Make a success of working with the other people in the office – learn how to get on with them and learn from them.

Your talent will show through and then you may be given more responsibility. At all times, you will need to prove yourself. You cannot expect your employer to know what you are capable of straight away, or to risk giving you tasks that you might fail to complete satisfactorily – that could result in problems for the company and an embarrassment for you. Remember the old adage: Learn to walk before you run.

Skills

All jobs need skills of one sort or another. Your first job will need few skills, but as you progress to more senior posts, more skills are needed. Job skills fall into two types: vocational or core skills.

Vocational skills

These are the skills that are linked to the actual job. When working in IT this could include:

- the ability to use a keyboard or mouse
- the ability to write computer programs
- the experience of using a word processing package
- the experience of using a desktop publishing package

ACTIVITY 9.11

List some vocational skills that you have acquired.

Key skills

These skills are useful for most jobs and include the ability:

- to think for yourself
- to work without supervision
- to work with numbers
- to solve problems
- to communicate your ideas to others
- to remember names and other important facts
- to work in a team
- to work to a deadline

ACTIVITY 9.12

Make a table with two columns and eight rows. Use the list of core skills above in the first column. Use the second column to write what level of skills you have in this area. Is there anything you can do to improve your levels of skills in these areas? Talk to your teacher/tutor if there are problems you need help to overcome, or if you need extra practice.

Qualifications

Most jobs now require the applicant to have some qualifications. Like skills, these split into two categories: vocational and academic.

Vocational qualifications

Vocational qualifications, which include GNVQs and NVQs, cover the types of tasks you do every day at work. Some example of vocational qualifications are:

- Foundation GNVQ in Information Technology
- RSA CLAIT (Computer Literacy and Information Technology)
- RSA II Keyboarding
- RSA II Databases
- NVQ

ACTIVITY 9.13

Write down what *vocational* qualifications you expect to have when you finish your course of study. This will be useful when preparing your CV.

Academic qualifications

Academic qualifications include GCSEs, and GCE A/AS levels qualifications. These are not directly related to a particular job. They might be studied at school or college before going to work, or going on to Higher Education. Examples include:

- GCSE English
- GCSE Science
- GCSE French
- GCSE History

ACTIVITY 9.14

Write down what *academic* qualifications you expect to have when you finish your course of study. Include the expected grades for each qualification. This will be useful when preparing your CV.

Advice and information

Always be willing to listen to others. People of all ages – younger and older – will have had different experiences from you, and hearing about them may help you. Before you can decide on whether to apply for a job, you need to know all about it:

- the purposes of the job
- the suitability of the job
- the availability of the job

Appropriate sources of information

All sources of information might be appropriate. It will be up to you to listen to everyone's views and decide whose advice helps you the most. There are three main sources, though, that you should consider:

- **Careers advisors** – these people will have more information to give you and may be specially trained to advise on careers.
- **Reference materials** – many books have been written offering job advice, and some include details of courses on offer, or organisations to contact.
- **Other informed sources** – such as staff in schools, people in industry involved in schools–industry link work, and personnel staff in industry.

We look at what sources you should use to find work in the IT industry in the next chapter.

The evidence indicators

To prove you have covered the material of this element you need to produce a presentation which:

- identifies two jobs that involve working with information technology which would suit you as initial employment and for further progression in the sector

- describes what is involved in each job and explaining why it would suit you
- identifies the main skills and qualifications required for each identified job
- identifies how you could obtain these skills and qualifications

Notes are also needed to show that you have sought advice and information from appropriate sources when necessary.

10 Plan for employment that involves working with information technology

This chapter covers the material needed for Element 3.3: Plan for employment that involves working with information technology.

The performance criteria state that the student must:

1. Identify **personal information** required to produce a curriculum vitae (CV) and produce a curriculum vitae (CV).
2. Describe the **main ways to find out** about job vacancies related to information technology.
3. Describe the **main stages in recruitment**.
4. Describe different **ways of presenting** personal information to prospective employers.
5. Seek **advice and information** from **appropriate sources** when necessary.

The knowledge range

To meet the performance criteria, you *must* cover the range. The words shown in bold in the performance criteria above highlight the skills and knowledge you will need and so we will now consider each of these in turn.

Personal information

An employer will ask you many questions about yourself before deciding whether to offer you a job. This is called personal information. Most of this information is written down, on your **CV (curriculum vitae)** or on an application form. To give the best possible impression, write your details as clearly as possible. On your CV, you should include:

- personal details
- subjects studied
- qualifications gained
- personal qualities
- experience and achievements gained through work and training
- any other achievements
- leisure activities

ACTIVITY 10.1

Prepare an outline CV, using the headings listed above. Prepare your CV on a word processing package so that you can amend it until you are happy with what it says. Later, you can amend it to keep it up-to-date.

Personal details

The basic details will be your name, address, age and gender (whether you are male or female). Nowadays, employers are not supposed to discriminate against applicants on the basis of the age or gender – or many other things – but it is useful for them to have this personal information about all applicants.

ACTIVITY 10.2

Complete the personal details section of your CV. Make sure the layout of the material is pleasing. Make sure that you have made no spelling or keying errors. The spelling checker will not know, for instance, if your surname is misspelt, and no prospective employer will be impressed if you made this kind of mistake!

Subjects studied

It is important to list subjects studied as well as qualifications achieved. Include details of the length of the course and where you were studying.

Qualifications

List your subjects in an order – either your favourite subjects first, or how well you have done, or in alphabetical order. At an interview, you may be asked to talk about the subjects you have studied and you may find it easier if you use this list as a prompt. It could be embarrassing if you could not remember which subjects you had been studying!

You may be asked to prove what qualifications you have achieved. It will be important to keep all certificates in a safe place. Do not send original certificates to a prospective employer; a photocopy could be sent in the post and then you could show them the original, if asked, at interview.

The information included so far is all factual. Be sure that what you write is true. If you are offered a job based on this information and then, later, the employer finds out it is not true, you could be dismissed.

ACTIVITY 10.3

Complete some more sections of your CV, and read back over the whole CV again. Have you missed any information out?

Personal qualities

You may write a paragraph about yourself. This information might be included on the CV or in a letter of application enclosed with the CV. Here is a checklist of questions you may want to consider:

- Are you always on time?
- Do you take care of your appearance?
- Can you get on well with others?
- Can you communicate your ideas to others?

- Are you polite?
- Are you friendly?
- Are you enthusiastic?
- Are you keen to learn new things?

If you are called for an interview, some of these personal qualities will be noted by your interviewer. Be sure to describe yourself honestly. The interviewer may notice if you behave differently from the impression given in your written application, and this will give him or her reason to doubt you.

ACTIVITY 10.4

Work with a friend on this activity. Each of you write a paragraph about yourself, ready to include in your CV or an application letter. Swap paragraphs and see if you agree with what has been written. Talk about what else you might write and then produce a revised version.

Experience and achievements gained through work and training

You might not appreciate how valuable work experience is, until you find that a prospective employer is impressed with what you have done. The teacher at school responsible for gaining a work placement should have tried to match you with your intended career path. If you enjoyed the work experience, you may have decided to follow that career path. More importantly, it may have helped you to decide what you did *not* like about certain working conditions, or opened your eyes as to what work is really like. Your prospective employer will know that you have already had a taste of work, and that is a good sign.

You may also have experienced particular tasks that will fall within your new job specification. This will help you to settle in more quickly.

You may have studied first aid or other useful basic skills at evening classes. Don't forget to include these on your CV.

Other achievements

Remember to mention other significant achievements, even if they didn't give you a special qualification.

- Were you a prefect at school?
- Did you get involved in school plays or musical production?
- How do you spend your free time? Do you help out with a youth club, or a guide or scout group?
- Do you do any voluntary work, e.g. at your church or a local hospital?
- Do you have a special skill, e.g. speak an unusual language, or do sign language?

ACTIVITY 10.5

Write short notes on your experience and achievements gained through work and training and any other achievements. Include relevant dates and times spent in training or on work experience. Add this information to your CV.

ACTIVITY 10.6

Do this activity with a partner. One person plays the part of an interviewer and, looking at the CV of the other, says: 'Tell me some more about your work experience.' The interviewee has to reply, and within a few sentences impress the interviewer. Can you remember what you have written on the CV? Can you add more details that will interest the prospective employer and impress them with what you have learnt through work experience?

Leisure activities

Leisure activities can be very active:

- football
- tennis
- running

Or not so active:

- walking

Or not active at all:

- chess
- reading
- stamp collecting

The importance of leisure activities was discussed in Chapter 9. Look back at the notes from Activity 9.7 and make sure you have included sufficient information to impress a prospective employer.

ACTIVITY 10.7

Complete your CV and print out a good copy. Show it to friends and teachers who may be able to offer advice as to how you could improve it. Listen to what they have to say, and make any alterations that you think will help. File your final CV in your portfolio.

The main ways to find out about job vacancies

There are four main sources of information about job vacancies:

- advertisements placed by employers seeking to recruit staff
- employers themselves, usually through their Personnel Department
- professional advisors, who make their living from matching job applicants to job vacancies
- informal sources, i.e. the 'grapevine'

Advertisements

Employers who need new staff usually place advertisements to attract applicants. Where they do this will depend on the type of job on offer, and the type of people they want to recruit.

- Employers seeking highly trained and highly experienced staff might approach an agency and ask them to 'headhunt' the right person for the job.
- Employers seeking well qualified people for job vacancies all over the country might use advertisements in the national press.
- Employers seeking people with special qualities might advertise in a specialist journal or trade magazine or in a supplement of a national newspaper.
- Employers seeking local staff might advertise through the local job centre, or use a notice board outside their own building. Lots of supermarkets do this.
- Sometimes jobs are advertised internally, to give existing staff the chance to seek promotion. People outside the company may not even be aware of these job opportunities.

ACTIVITY 10.8

Look back at the advertisements you collected for Activity 9.1. You should have noted which publications you took them from. Does the pattern of advertising match that explained previously.

Employers

You could contact employers direct. By keeping watch on which companies are recruiting, i.e. which ones are advertising for staff, you could contact them directly and say you are enquiring about other vacancies in their organisation.

You may persuade them to accept a copy of your CV to keep on file should a suitable vacancy arise. Certainly, you may find they appreciate how keen you are to obtain a job. If they decide to interview you for a vacancy, it may save them the costs of advertising.

In the first instance, you might contact the Personnel Department, but you might also try the IT Department. When you telephone a company, speak to the switchboard operator and ask who you should speak to about vacancies. Ask for the name of the person in charge of recruitment, and then ask to be put through to them. Make a note of their name and be sure to make every effort to impress them when you do get through.

This method requires perseverence; it is like looking for a needle in a haystack – a job in a company that has not advertised a vacancy. But if you decide you like the way a company works, it is worth approaching them. For every ten refusals, you might get someone to put your CV on file. For every ten CVs you send, you might get one interview. For every ten interviews, you might get one offer of a job. Then all your hard work will have been worth it.

Professional advisors

Professional advisors earn their living by advising others on how to get a job. These include careers teachers, and staff at job centres and employment bureaux. These people deal with enquiries all day from people like you. They have all the necessary information at their fingertips:

- details of local companies
- contacts within those companies

- details of further training courses that might help you to break into a particular line of work

You might also talk to people with IT qualifications who are already working in the IT industry. They may be able to give you some very valuable advice, and perhaps the names of some contacts within companies that might employ someone like you.

Informal sources

You will hear people say: "It's not what you know. It's who you know that counts." Another favourite is: "I was in the right place at the right time."

If you think you don't know anyone who counts, or you feel you are the one in the wrong place at the wrong time, this news is not encouraging.

However, you may be surprised what contacts you do have. Through family and friends, you may know someone, who knows someone, who knows someone who can help. The trick is to let friends and family know that you are looking for work in a particular area, and to behave in such a way that they would be pleased to pass your name on. It is unlikely that you will receive any help from these informal contacts if people worry about you letting them down.

Main stages in recruitment

There are definite stages in the recruitment process.

ACTIVITY 10.9

Before reading through this section, write short notes on what you understand these terms to mean:

job vacancy	appointment
job description	record of achievement
job offer	interview
advertisement	selection
application	shortlist

The job description

The employer sets out a **job description** of the vacancy. This is a written description of the tasks and responsibilities of the person taking on the job. It may include details such as conditions of working (i.e. hours of working), holiday arrangements, place of work, persons immediately above or below the job position, and so on.

The advertisement

Usually an **advertisement** is placed. This will invite suitable applicants to apply for the job. The advertisement should include several details:

- the name of the employer
- the place of work
- the type of work or job title
- some idea about pay and conditions
- details of how to apply, e.g. an address or telephone number and a person to contact

ACTIVITY 10.10

Look back at the advertisements collected in activities in Chapter 9. Do they all include the types of information listed above? For each advertisement, would you know what information to send, where to send it, and to whom it should be addressed?

Applying for the job

Applicants apply for the job. They may write a **letter of application** to the company and enclose a copy of their **CV**.

The employer may expect to receive many applications for one post. To ensure they have exactly the information they require each applicant may be sent an **application form**. This is a questionnaire which has to be completed and sent back to the company before the application will be considered any further. Often the application form duplicates information already given on the CV, but you must complete it, to make the job of selecting (and rejecting) applicants easier for the employer.

ACTIVITY 10.11

Do this activity with a partner. Each of you write a letter of application for one of the jobs you have seen advertised. (If you have not yet seen a job advertisement that you would apply for, imagine that you have the required qualifications for one.) Produce your letter of application in your own handwriting. Swap letters and consider whether you would be impressed enough to invite this applicant for interview. Discuss ways of improving the letter.

Shortlisting

The employer has to decide who to interview – a **shortlist** of applicants is drawn up.

- Some applications will be rejected straight away because their qualifications do not match the job description.
- Some will be rejected because the company has a limit on the number of people they are willing to interview (for cost and/or time reasons).

It is at this stage that the overall effect of your application form and your CV and your covering letter of application will be all-important. The time spent deciding whether to put your application into the 'yes' or 'no' pile may be only a matter of minutes. Once put into the 'no' pile, you will have lost your chance to impress that particular employer. It is therefore very important that everything you send is of the highest quality in appearance and content.

ACTIVITY 10.12

Have another look at your CV and your letter of application. Have you included all relevant details? Would you be one of the short-listed applicants. If not, what can you do to improve your chances of success?

The interview process

A **shortlist** of applicants will be invited for interview. How the interview takes place will vary from employer to employer. Some large organisations offer an 'open day' for a large number of potential recruits. This involves a talk from a senior manager, a tour of the offices and probably handing out some literature to answer any questions the applicants might have. Some applicants will then decide they do not want to work for the company and **de-select** themselves. This makes the next stage of interviewing less time-consuming for the employer. They only have applicants who are keen to work for them.

Most interviews involve a **selection panel** – it may be one person, or two or three people – who will meet each applicant, look through the information received to date and then ask more questions to help them to decide who should be offered the job.

It is said that people make up their minds about someone they meet within the first few seconds, sometimes even before that person speaks. Good interviewers will be aware of this, but if you use those first few seconds well you may have won half the interview battle before you have even sat down. If you manage to disappoint the interviewer in the same few seconds, you will have difficulty winning back his or her confidence.

ACTIVITY 10.13

Look back at your notes from Activity 9.8. If possible, work in a group for this role play activity. Two or three people are needed for the selection panel. One person (take it in turns) is the interviewee. Others observe and make notes on what is said and done. It helps if you can video the whole interview and then look back over everyone's performance. Set the selection panel behind a long table with one chair in front for the interviewee. Ask the interviewee to wait outside the door (an imaginary one, if necessary) until invited in. Watch the interviewee walk in, sit down and answer the first few questions. Include statements like:

- Did you find us all right?
- Tell me some more about yourself.
- What makes you think you would be suitable for this job?

Watch the interviewee for subconscious movements: fiddling with hair, chewing nails, fidgeting – these all indicate nervousness and can be negative signs. How well does the interviewee inform the panel of plus points? How quickly does he or she impress the panel? Does the interviewee do anything that would *not* impress the panel?

Limit each 'interview' to five minutes. The first time you see yourself on video may not be a pleasant experience, but this activity is exceptionally good practice for a real interview.

Selection

Once all the interviews have taken place, the selection panel will meet to discuss all the applicants and to decide who, if anyone, is to be **offered** the post. This may happen straight away, or there may be a delay if information still has to arrive, e.g. references from previous employers.

Appointment

The successful applicant will be offered the post. This may be a verbal communication, but should be followed up by a formal letter offering the post. The applicant then needs to accept the post in writing. Final details on a starting date and the salary will be agreed at this stage. The applicant has then been **appointed**.

ACTIVITY 10.14

Look back at your notes from Activity 10.9. Revise these notes in light of what you have learnt. Draw a diagram to show the events involved in recruiting new staff. Use colour to show where you, the applicant, have an opportunity to impress the prospective employer. Notice the stages at which you may be rejected, and make notes on how you can avoid this.

Ways of presenting

You have several opportunities to present yourself to a prospective employer. To begin with, you may telephone to enquire about the vacancy. Then you may:

- write a letter of application
- fill in an application form
- present your CV
- present your record of achievement, e.g. the National Record of Achievement

All these are written forms of communication. Finally, if you are successful in being called for interview, you will have the opportunity to present yourself personally. The impression you give visually and the way you conduct yourself during the interview will be judged.

ACTIVITY 10.15

Look back at all your notes from this chapter. Are there any ways you can improve your presentation? Can you improve your CV? Do you need more interview practice? Talk to your teacher/tutor if you feel you need help.

Advice and information

In Chapter 9, we looked at sources of advice and information. As part of the evidence needed for this element, you must demonstrate that you have sought advice:

- on vacancies
- on skills needed
- on further training needed
- on training opportunities

You are expected to have used **appropriate sources** of advice and information, such as:

- careers advisors
- reference materials
- other informed sources, e.g. staff in schools and in industry involved in schools–industry link work, personnel staff in industry

ACTIVITY 10.16

Refer to your notes. What advice have you sought, and who did you approach for help? Annotate your notes to show where you have listened to others, and whether or not you decided to take their advice.

By now you should have more idea on what you might want to do when you finish this course. You may, at least, be clearer about what you do *not* want to do, or what you will not be able to do without further qualifications.

ACTIVITY 10.17

If you have not yet applied for any jobs, or made a decision about further training, do so now. Select a company to apply to for a job, or an establishment to apply for a place on a training course. Seek advice from all sources available to you, and keep a record of this.

The evidence indicators

To prove you have covered the material of this element, you need to produce a CV outlining your personal information.

A summary is also needed, describing:

- the main ways to find out about job vacancies related to information technology
- the main stages in recruitment
- different ways in which personal information is presented to prospective employers.

Notes are needed:

- identifying the personal information required to produce a CV
- showing that you have sought advice and information from appropriate sources when necessary

Wordsearch 3

These words were used in Unit 3, find them in this wordsearch:

ACADEMIC
ACCURACY
ACHIEVEMENTS
ADDRESS
ADVICE
AGE
APPLY
APPOINT

CAREERS ADVISOR
CORE
CV
EMPLOYER
EMPLOYMENT
GENDER
GNVQ
INFORMATION

INTERVIEW
JOBDESCRIPTION
JOBS
MANUAL
NAME
QUALIFICATIONS
QUALITIES
REFERENCE

RESPONSIBILITY
SELECTION
SKILL
SPEED
TASK
TRAIN
VOCATIONAL

R	O	S	I	V	D	A	S	R	E	E	R	A	C	S
N	E	T	E	C	I	V	D	A	G	E	N	R	N	C
A	C	S	M	A	N	U	A	L	A	N	O	O	S	V
M	I	A	P	P	L	Y	A	E	Q	U	I	W	L	S
E	M	P	L	O	Y	E	R	R	U	T	T	E	A	T
R	E	P	O	S	N	K	T	O	A	R	A	I	N	N
S	D	O	Y	P	R	S	S	C	L	A	M	V	O	E
E	A	I	M	E	D	E	I	A	I	I	R	R	I	M
L	C	N	E	E	E	F	D	B	T	N	O	E	T	E
E	A	T	N	D	I	E	Q	N	I	X	F	T	A	V
C	G	W	T	L	L	I	K	S	E	L	N	N	C	E
T	N	L	A	D	D	R	E	S	S	G	I	I	O	I
I	V	U	R	E	F	E	R	E	N	C	E	T	V	H
O	Q	S	B	O	J	A	C	C	U	R	A	C	Y	C
N	O	I	T	P	I	R	C	S	E	D	B	O	J	A

Sample test for Unit 3

Check that you have understood the material of this unit by doing these sample external test questions.

These questions have been based on questions set by two of the three awarding bodies for GNVQ: RSA and City & Guilds. The questions set by BTEC are similar.

Each question offers four options, but only one of them is correct. At the end of this book, the correct answers are given.

Read each question very carefully before making your decision.

Question 1 Which ONE of the following would be most likely to use EFTPOS (electronic funds transfer at point-of-sale) as part of their job role?

a   video games programmer
b   word processing operator
c   shop till cashier
d   cheque card manufacturer

Question 2 A job involving CAM (computer-aided manufacture) would be most likely to be done by a:

a   planning engineer
b   bank clerk
c   senior gardener
d   dairy farmer

Question 3 In which ONE of the following is a light pen most likely to be used to read bar codes on books?

a   a church
b   a cinema
c   a library
d   a travel agency

Question 4 Which ONE of the following organisations is most likely to use a computerised booking system?

a   church
b   cinema
c   library
d   travel agent

Question 5   Which ONE of the following is a benefit of using an IT system to produce a long letter rather than handwriting it?

a   redrafting is slower
b   accuracy is guaranteed
c   redrafting is easier
d   confidentiality is maintained

Question 6   The Post Office use automated machinery to sort mail by reading the postcode. Which ONE of the following is a benefit of using this process?

a   faster sorting
b   guaranteed delivery
c   reduced postal rate
d   fewer mail vans

Question 7   The wages of a company are paid in cash. Each pay envelope has the correct notes and coins placed in it by hand. Which ONE of the following describes this process?

a   automated
b   electrified
c   manual
d   textual

Question 8   An applicant for the job of a word processor operator should be:

a   an able programmer
b   a first class engineer
c   a competent telephonist
d   a fast and accurate typist

Question 9   Which ONE of the following is a core skill which would be needed for a user to set up a spreadsheet?

a   knowledge of a foreign language
b   a good level of numeracy
c   flexible working hours
d   word processing experience

Question 10   Which ONE of the following tasks would normally be done by a database operator?

a   inserting names and addresses
b   deleting the program
c   mending the computer's hardware
d   multiplying figures and entering formula

Question 11   Which ONE of the following should be contacted for information about training courses?

a   insurance advisor
b   careers advisor
c   holiday advisor
d   hardware advisor

Question 12   To find out if there are any vacancies for software programmers in the local area, a person should visit:

a   a computer retailer
b   a hardware specialist
c   an assembly line
d   a job centre

Question 13   Which ONE of the following should an applicant for a job include on a CV?

a   the applicant's brother's and sister's names
b   the applicant's grandparent's address
c   the applicant's parent's birthdays
d   the applicant's name and address

Question 14   A CV should contain an applicant's:

a   date of birth
b   date of operation
c   date of purchase
d   date of death

Question 15   Which ONE of the following would a prospective employer expect to see on a CV?

a   examinations not attempted
b   results of internal tests
c   number of school detentions
d   qualifications achieved

Question 16   A CV should contain details of a person's:

a   pets
b   friends
c   dislikes
d   age

Question 17   Which ONE of the following people should be contacted to find out about job vacancies in the computer department of a company?

a   the production manager
b   the canteen manager
c   the personnel manager
d   the transport manager

Question 18   Information about job vacancies would be found in:

a   work sheets
b   advertisements
c   application letters
d   programming manuals

Question 19   Information about unfilled positions in a local supermarket are likely to be displayed on:

a   the vacancies notice board
b   the staff social calendar
c   the special offers list
d   the opening and closing times poster

Question 20   An employer looking for staff may:

a   write a letter of engagement
b   place an advertisement
c   compile a personnel list
d   send a notice of payment

Question 21   A vacancy exists for a data entry clerk. Which ONE of the following would describe the tasks involved in this job?

a   job grading
b   person specification
c   job description
d   pay slip

Question 22   If a firm is interested in talking to an applicant about their application for a job

a   the applicant will be offered training
b   the applicant will be given careers advice
c   the applicant will be invited for interview
d   the applicant will be asked to attend an award ceremony

Question 23   If an applicant is successful at interview the company will offer

    a   an appointment
    b   an award
    c   an examination
    d   an investigation

Question 24   Which ONE of the following is shown in Text A?

    a   a CV
    b   a letter of application
    c   an application form
    d   a record of achievement

Text A

2nd July 1996

                       12 High Street
                       Anytownwhere
                       Countyside

Dear Sirs,

I am writing to apply for the post of data entry clerk as advertised in the Western Informer on 30th June.

Please send me more information about this vacancy.

Yours faithfully,

Julie Phillips

Question 25   A person who is applying for a job might be asked to complete:

    a   an application form
    b   a driving licence
    c   an insurance form
    d   a provisional licence

Question 26   Which ONE of the following would usually be included with an application form?

    a   a personal reference
    b   a national record of achievement (NRA)
    c   a letter of acceptance
    d   a curriculum vitae (CV)

Question 27   On leaving, most students receive from their school or college:

    a   a cheque book
    b   a letter of application
    c   a record of achievement
    d   a letter of progress

Question 28   A junior clerk wants to be promoted to section leader. Which ONE of the following would be recommended by the personnel manager for this promotion?

    a   a reduction in working hours
    b   six weeks of community service
    c   a course of further training
    d   a period of voluntary work

Question 29   Reference materials about training course opportunities can be found in:

    a   a newsagent
    b   a health centre
    c   a careers centre
    d   a railway station

Answers to sample test questions

These sample test questions should have been easy for you to answer correctly. Use this table to see where you might have gone wrong.

Question	Unit 1	Unit 2	Unit 3	Questions	Unit 1	Unit 2	Unit 3
1	d	b	c	17	a	d	c
2	c	c	a	18	b	a	b
3	a	b	c	19	b	d	a
4	b	d	d	20	a	c	b
5	c	a	c	21	c	b	c
6	c	c	a	22	d	c	c
7	b	d	c	23	b	b	a
8	d	d	d	24	c	a	b
9	c	b	b	25	c	d	a
10	a	b	a	26	a	b	d
11	b	b	b	27	c	b	c
12	a	b	d	28	b	c	c
13	b	d	d	29	c	c	c
14	b	c	a	30	b		
15	d	d	d	31	c		
16	c	b	d				

Answers to wordsearches

Wordsearch 1

```
D I S P L A Y R A R O P M E T
R N P E O M O R R R R P R K E
A V R F R M S A O I I A P N L
O O E X T U D E N T W A O A E
B I A N N I T T S T C H H B T
Y C D O O I E P F A P A S B E
E I S I C R O O A E B K F A X
K N H S K T S T L C S A V T T
S G E I C I S E A T A D T O P
R B E V O S T R E S U O M A T
O A T E T I B E D T C E R I D
S C M L S T N E N A M R E P J
N S A E T Y R A I L I X U A T
E N E T W O R K G R A P H I C
S G N I S S E C O R P D R O W
```

Wordsearch 2

```
E G F O R I E N T A T I O N D
L R I R E M B O L D E N M M A
B A L E C A A I A E X C N U T
A P E T T R T T E L T O S L A
T H N C A G E A O E I P C O B
K I A A N I G L D T L Y O C A
T C M R G N A U A E A Y L O S
I U E A L U M C E N N L O P E
A T L H E N I L R E D N U Z N
R R L C C F P A F L S A R Y H
T E I A I L I C O I C O A C F
R B F T Y R L N O F A R R L I
O M S D R O C E R B P A S T E
P U S N D W U L P S E E N I L
J N F O R M A T E S F O N T D
```

Wordsearch 3

R	O	S	I	V	D	A	S	R	E	E	R	A	C	S
N	E	T	E	C	I	V	D	A	G	E	N	R	N	C
A	C	S	M	A	N	U	A	L	A	N	O	O	S	V
M	I	A	P	P	L	Y	A	E	Q	U	I	W	L	S
E	M	P	L	O	Y	E	R	R	U	T	T	E	A	T
R	E	P	O	S	N	K	T	O	A	R	A	I	N	N
S	D	O	Y	P	R	S	S	C	L	A	M	V	O	E
E	A	I	M	E	D	E	I	A	I	I	R	R	I	M
L	C	N	E	E	F	D	B	T	N	O	E	T	E	E
E	A	T	N	D	I	E	Q	N	I	X	F	T	A	V
C	G	W	T	L	L	I	K	S	E	L	N	N	C	E
T	N	L	A	D	D	R	E	S	S	G	I	I	O	I
I	V	U	R	E	F	E	R	E	N	C	E	T	V	H
O	Q	S	B	O	J	A	C	C	U	R	A	C	Y	C
N	O	I	T	P	I	R	C	S	E	D	B	O	J	A

Abbreviations

ATM	automatic teller machine
BACS	bankers automated clearing services
BBC	British Broadcasting Corporation
CAD	computer-aided design
CV	curriculum vitae
DTP	desktop publishing
EFT	electronic funds transfer
EFTPOS	electronic funds transfer at point-of-sale
fax	facsimile
GCSE	General Certificate of Secondary Education
GNVQ	General National Vocational Qualification
ID	identity
IT	information technology
JANET	Joint Academic Network
LCD	liquid crystal display
NI	National Insurance
NLQ	near letter quality
NRA	National Record of Achievement
PAYE	pay as you earn
PC	performance criteria
RAM	random access memory
ROM	read only memory
RSA	Royal Society of Arts
tab	tabulation
TV	television
UK	United Kingdom
VAT	value added tax
VDU	visual display unit
WYSIWYG	what you see is what you get

Index

Also available from Addison Wesley Longman

Intermediate GNVQ Information Technology Assignment Pack
John Holland
ISBN 0-582-29335-9

Written specifically for the latest Intermediate GNVQ Information Technology specification, these assignments follow the GNVQ structure exactly and cover all four mandatory units, and the four BTEC optional units.

Already tried and tested, the pack provide lecturers with a time-saving photocopiable resource, enabling more time to be spent on the delivery on the delivery to students. These evidence gathering assignments also include sample test questions to prepare students fully for unit tests. The integration of the GNVQ key skills into the assignments ensures students have a balanced approach to gaining evidence.

Intermediate GNVQ Information Technology
Tina Cross & Collette Jones
ISBN 0-582-29226-3

This lively and easy-to-read text has been written specifically to provide a one-stop source covering all four mandatory units at this level. It follows the GNVQ structure and makes the text easy to follow by breaking down each element into the individual range categories. The practical activities included throughout provide ample material for students to test their knowledge and comprehension. Case studies illustrate the theory with real-life situations to consolidate learning.

A Glossary of Computing Terms–8th edition
The British Computer Society
ISBN 0-582-27544-X

Published in 1995, this new edition of a well-established and popular glossary explains over 1800 computer terms in simple language with numerous illustrations to aid comprehension. It has been reorganized into three main parts: how computer systems are used; what computer systems are made up of; and how computer systems work. Over 40 essays have been included to illustrate how terms can be used with a written context. It provides a standardized interpretation of computing terminology and is an essential guide for students, home users and all those involved with computer science, technology, business and management.

Foundation GNVQ Core Skills: Communication
Desmond W. Evans
ISBN 0-582-29297-2

This text comprehensively meets the needs of all students following the new GNVQ Core Skills specification. The book follows the sequence of elements and performance criteria for easy reference and student self-directed study. Students are provided with detailed guidance on how to develop communication expertise and practical skills, as well as how to use such techniques in providing integrated or self-contained portfolio activities. Each chapter includes detailed explanations of current principles and practices, as well as sets of skill- and portfolio-building activities, discussion topics and self-test review questions (with answers).

For further information about these and other titles, or to order a copy, please contact:

Longman Customer Information Centre,
PO Box 88,
Harlow, Essex
CM19 5SR

Telephone: 01279 623928
Fax: 01279 414130